CRISIS IN EDUCATION

Public education a disaster
...but there's new hope for parents.

Donald R. Howard, Ph.D.

CRISIS IN EDUCATION

Public education a disaster
...but there's new hope for parents.

Donald R. Howard, Ph.D.
with H. Edward Rowe

New Leaf
Press

FIRST EDITION
1990

Library of Congress Catalog Card Number: 90-62699
ISBN: 0-89221-185-7

DEDICATION

Dedicated to the pastors, parents, and Christian workers who have sacrificed to protect precious children from the academic perils of Western culture.

CONTENTS

FOREWORD

In the preface of his book titled *Against the Night*, Chuck Colson warns that "a crisis of immense proportion is upon us." He explains that the real crisis is "...in the character of our culture, where values that restrain inner vices and develop inner virtues are eroding."

The most astute observers of our time are agreed that a serious and continuing erosion of values threatens our nation and civilization.

In early America a Theologically-based value system was perpetuated through character training, which occurred as an inseparable part of education. But tragically, as this book will show, a sweeping Humanist revolution brought drastic changes.

The control of education passed from families to government-funded bureaucracy. God was expelled summarily from the educational system. Into the vacuum created by the expulsion of God, there rushed a polluted stream of atheistic philosophy, situational ethics, values-neutral curricula, sex education, and advocacy of a variety of immoral "lifestyle" choices.

Then the wreckage began washing up on the shore—evident in the form of plunging test scores, moral decay, sexual idolatry, gang wars, burgeoning crime, crowded prisons, a holocaust of sexually transmitted diseases, and general economic and social chaos.

These developments have now catapulted our society, including our system of government-sponsored education, into times of unprecedented crisis.

The purpose of this book is to address the current crisis in education. We will trace its background as the consequence of a departure from the Theistic roots of our culture. We will relate the advent, eventual dominance, and bitter fruits of Secular Humanism in relation to education and our society as a whole.

Finally, we will describe God's better way, as embodied in His clearly revealed program for education. We will conclude by showing how current trends in Christian education are bringing new hope to parents through dynamic educational services and growing influence on a global scale.

Samuel Johnson, the famous English writer of the eighteenth century, capsulized the purpose of education in a single sentence. ''The supreme end of education,'' wrote Johnson, ''is expert discernment in all things--the power to tell the good from the bad, the genuine from the counterfeit, and to prefer the good and genuine to the bad and the counterfeit.''

Effective training in how to distinguish good from evil, and in performance of the good in preference to the evil, is at once the missing ingredient in government education and the superlative contribution of Christian education.

This book is sent forth with the prayer that it will foster a better understanding of the current crisis in education, that it will ignite a bright new fire of hope in the breast of every concerned parent, and that it will provide guidance for family and private-sector initiatives designed to resolve the crisis.

GODLY FOUNDATIONS

Historians tell us we can better understand contemporary events by understanding the past. A review of the significant influences that gave our culture its starting point will help us to interpret changes and trends that brought us to the crisis in education which we are experiencing today.

The chart on page 17 identifies the period we call the *Beginning of Western Greatness.* Starting in the 1630's, the Pilgrims and Puritans brought the English Awakening to the Western Hemisphere through a movement of Godly people from Europe to the New World. Their purpose was to establish a place in which they could enjoy freedom of religion.

The Pilgrim and Puritan forefathers founded Western culture on Biblical principles. The *philosophy* was Theism, or God-centered beliefs relating to all areas of life.

The first school law, in 1642, required parents to provide three areas of teaching in their educational programs:
- Reading and writing
- The laws of the land
- *Religion*

It may be difficult to imagine today that the teaching of *religion* was required by law in early America. The first teachers were pastors, and the first schools were in churches. The first textbook was the Bible.

Another *public school law* was passed in 1647. It required communities of fifty or more families to provide education for those who could not afford it: namely, the poor. From this beginning, ninety-five percent of the youngsters attended private schools, and five percent attended public schools.

This ratio was virtually unchanged for the next two centuries.

In all the schools, private and public, there were three prevailing presuppositions that gave foundation and force to Western culture:
- God exists and gives man a sense of responsibility;
- *God created* us, giving us a sense of accountability for our lives; and
- *God has spoken*, giving us a sense of reality based on His Word.

BEGINNING of
WESTERN GREATNESS

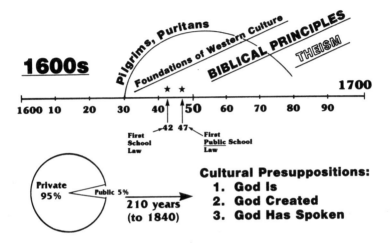

1600s

Pilgrims, Puritans
Foundations of Western Culture
BIBLICAL PRINCIPLES
THEISM

1700

1600 10   20   30   40 50   60   70   80   90

★ ★

→42 47↘

First
School
Law

First
Public School
Law

Private
95%

Public 5%

210 years
(to 1840)

Cultural Presuppositions:
1. **God Is**
2. **God Created**
3. **God Has Spoken**

This active *Theism* was at the root of Western culture as a positive God-centered philosophy. This is not to say that all men who lived at that time were God-fearing Bible believers and that there were not abuses. It simply means that society in general had a philosophy of belief in God.

This Theistic belief affected commerce, ethics, morality, domestic activities, and national policy. This Godly consensus directed the nation's judiciary, military, educational, governmental, civil, and economic leadership.

Theistic Cultural Consensus

By the 1700s a growing number of immigrants came to the American colonies. The Theistic cultural consensus was then diluted by other values the newcomers brought with them. The people had a "frontier morality," which permitted all kinds of harshness and wrongdoing. Historians wrote that by 1730 most church members were not "born again." The new generation did not have the piety and morals of the original colonists.

A small number of great pulpit speakers began to address the growing concern with this issue of moral backsliding. Their activities created a spiritual hunger for the former influences of the passing Theistic consensus.

In the 1730s, in Pennsylvania, Dutch reformer Theodore Frelinghuysen preached fiery revival sermons that resulted in vast numbers of conversions.

In New England, Jonathan Edwards preached about a literal hell and damnation. He sought to convince sinners to seek forgiveness and regeneration. Jonathan Edwards' hard-hitting sermons took an uncompromising stand against baptism for church membership of persons who were not "born again." For this, Edwards was driven from his pulpit and became an itinerant preacher-evangelist.

John and Charles Wesley came to America and preached the need for individual conversion. So did English Methodist preacher George Whitefield.

These men were so effective that revival broke out across the new nation, and the cultural consensus returned to Biblical principles in what historians call the Great Awakening.

Great Awakening

It was this generation that laid the foundation for the birth of America. By 1776 the Declaration of Independence was drafted, incorporating those essential Biblical presuppositions of the 1600s.

In 1787 the Constitution declared other basic Biblical principles, setting forth a democratic, representative form of government—the first of its kind in world history.

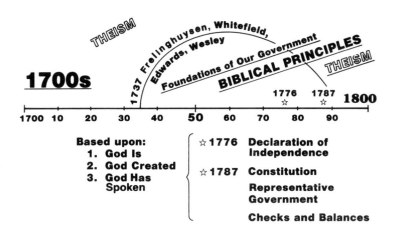

19

The Great Awakening and its influence on America's origins have provided, for this Republic, the most profound expression of liberty for the largest number of people over the longest period of time in all of the world's history.

In very simple terms, the reason we are free to buy land, build our own home upon it, create a business, or even invest in a religious enterprise, is because of Biblical influences on the development of American government.

Although it is not reported in most history textbooks, early American leaders sought God's wisdom, guidance, and favor at every turn. They debated, to be sure, but they also *prayed*—individually and corporately.

In the Mayflower Compact and throughout every other early American document, a dependence on Almighty God was not just acknowledged; it was *practiced*.

The Great Awakening of the 1700s reestablished our Theistic Western culture in America.

Second Awakening

By the 1800s this new experiment called "liberty" was working so well it attracted an even greater groundswell of immigrants than had come a century earlier. Most of them came from Europe where Godly values were in decline. The Industrial Revolution was then underway in America, and the nation was basking in the economic growth and self-sufficiency that eventually produced conflict and excesses.

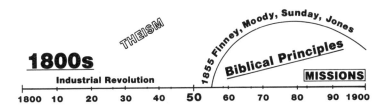

At this time a young attorney began to preach in factories near his home in Ohio. Factory owners even shut down plants and brought their workers together to hear young Charles Finney preach about the need to repent from sin and seek God.

Since most of his life was lived before the Civil War, Finney was an outspoken critic of slavery. He insisted that it was impossible ''to be on the right side of God and the wrong side of slavery'' at the same time.

Ironically, Finney's parents were not Christians, so his education had offered virtually no religious instruction.

However, in young Charles' studies of elementary law, he continually found references to the Scriptures as the authority for many of the principles of common law. This led the inquisitive law student to study the Bible and attend church. Following his investigation of God's Word, Charles

Finney became a believer. Then he began witnessing to others concerning what God had done in his life. These experiences soon gave way to revival meetings where Finney preached, and countless thousands came to Jesus Christ in repentance.

Following in Finney's footsteps was another evangelist reared in New England. Young Dwight L. Moody left home in the middle of the nineteenth century at age nineteen with plans and goals to make a fortune.

He traveled first to Boston to sell shoes. There a Sunday school teacher, Ed Kimball, shared the gospel with young Moody, and the young man became a Christian. Then he traveled west to the wild frontier town of Chicago.

In Chicago, during the second half of the 1800s, D. L. Moody effectively preached the need for repentance and personal salvation. His meetings grew in size and scope.

By 1885 Moody began to focus on church leadership and felt a strong responsibility to establish foreign missions. He believed it was possible to evangelize the entire world by the end of the nineteenth century. Consequently, the great Missionary Era was born.

By the end of the century and the first few decades of the twentieth century, his vision was picked up by others. It was during this period that many of the great itinerant evangelists became known: Billy Sunday, Sam Jones, Mordecai Ham, and Bob Jones.

This period of American history has been called the *Second Great Awakening*. This time a Theistic philosophy and consensus not only reformed the nation but also took on an international status. Foreign nations saw in the freedom-loving people of America ("the good Yanks") the role models for leadership and respect. Wherever these people went in the world with the Bible and their religious influence, Western culture was extended.

However, not all the voices proclaimed Godly values and a Theistic philosophy. A few dissident, radical voices outside the Theistic cultural consensus were vocal enough to have an influence not only in America but throughout Western civilization.

These voices would provide the foundation for our contemporary crisis in education. We turn next to a review of some of the more prominent philosophical thinking that provided the soil in which this crisis was to grow.

ROOTS OF MODERN EDUCATION

During the nineteenth century, the seeds of unbelief began to sprout and spread throughout Western culture. It was during this period that a succession of dominant philosophers arose to influence the thinking of Western men.

Six Radical Thinkers

Robert Owen

One of the first radical voices to be raised against the Theistic consensus was that of a Welshman, Robert Owen. Owen was an educator and an atheist who came to America in 1813.

He preached that man is not responsible for his own character, that it is shaped by his environment and society. Owen also taught that religion and capitalism made men evil through superstition and competition. His ideas were promoted widely by a coalition of Harvard-Unitarian forces which sought "salvation" through an educational system free of both religion and capitalism. Owen even gave educators a new means to achieve those purposes. He dubbed his scheme a "social science."

Social science, to Robert Owen, meant the use of education as a scientific tool for radical reform of human character. It would be a totalitarian program: all people would eventually be included through state-run compulsory education. This idea was a drastic departure from the past. Up to this time in America's history, ninety-five percent of the students attended private or church-run schools controlled and financed by the parents locally.

The Harvard-Unitarian intellectuals applauded and implemented the radical reform concept. They began indoctrinating school children in the new idea that they should be loyal to the *state*, rather than to their parents. Compulsory education had to be created to purge the new generation of all "superstitions" related to religion and the "evils" of capitalism.

Robert Owen was called "the father of modern socialism." He bought a parcel of ground in Indiana on the Wabash River and established a commune called New Harmony. It was a prototype of a socialist community.

But when public criticism arose, the "Owenites'' (as they were called) organized into secret cells to continue their aims. Since Owen's ideas were not well received in America, he returned to Europe, where he succeeded in transforming the entire school system of Prussia from religion-based education to a government-run system.

Horace Mann

In 1827 a teacher by the name of Horace Mann failed in his first year of teaching. Mann went back to college, studied law, and became an attorney. Later, he was elected to the Massachusetts Board of Education and by 1837 was appointed secretary of the state board of education.

Mann visited Prussia to see the system of government-operated schools created by Robert Owen. The concept so excited Mann that he came back to America to fashion Owen's radical experiment as a model for New England schools.

Mann referred to this new educational model as ''progressive,'' and it watered the first seeds of *government education* on American soil.

Horace Mann is called ''the father of public education.'' He no doubt got his reputation because government-financed public schools began to flourish in our nation following the Civil War. Horace Mann is, in reality, the father of American *governmental* education.

The number of children attending the private, parent-controlled-and-financed schools shifted downward from ninety-five percent to ninety percent by 1850, with ten percent of students then enrolled in tax-supported public schools.

Many people, even today, think that a free, public, *government* education is guaranteed in the U.S. Constitution. The fact is, education is not even mentioned in the Constitution. Education was one of the rights "reserved to the people."

Compulsory secular education designed to purge the "superstitions of religion" from the cultural consensus gained momentum in America during the latter half of the nineteenth century.

But Mann's ideas drew sharp criticism from the clergy. One leading minister predicted, "If we do what Mann wants us to do with our schools, we will create the greatest tool for the advancement of atheism that the world has ever seen."

Charles Darwin

In 1859 Charles Darwin wrote a book titled *On the Origin of Species by Means of Natural Selection*. It introduced a new idea—*evolution*. It expounded the idea that variation, struggle for survival, and natural selection were the "means adopted by the Creator to populate the earth."

Ironically, Darwin received his training at Christ College in Cambridge as a preparation for the Anglican ministry. He never intended that his ideas should undermine faith in God. He wrote his book as an explanation of how God created life.

Nevertheless, when Darwin later proposed the theory that life began by chance combinations of chemicals, light, and energy, intellectual atheists leaped to embrace it. Here, at last, was a *basic world-view of origins* that *did not* depend upon a Creator God.

Karl Marx

In 1867 Karl Marx, an atheist, attempted to build upon Darwin's theory of evolution.

In his book *Das Kapital*, Marx attempted to apply Darwin's view of evolutionary struggle among forms of animal life as a *universal* concept to explain all of life's disciplines. He taught that "survival of the fittest" also applies to government and society.

In *Das Kapital*, Marx contended that government systems evolved out of the feudal states to capitalism and then eventually to the utopia of socialism. Marx wanted to dedicate his book to Darwin, who declined his offer.

Marx said humanity would be free to control its own destiny only when socialism replaced capitalism. His views set the stage for the great political struggles to follow in the next century.

Friedrich Nietzsche

In 1882 a German philosopher, Friedrich Nietzsche, began to write that God was dead, or at least distant. In his writing, *The Will to Power* (published by his sister after his death), Nietzsche taught that man would triumph over his own destiny, that mankind lived in a universe ruled by scientific laws and therefore had no need of the "superstition" of the Bible, God, or religion.

Both Marx and Nietzsche were preaching the same thoughts which had also been expressed earlier by the extreme radical Theologian-philosophers G. W. F. Hegel and Friedrich Engels.

By the end of the nineteenth century a chorus of other radical voices in the intellectual circles of Europe arose in agreement.

Sigmund Freud

Sigmund Freud (1856-1939) wrote *The Interpretation of Dreams*, which was built on "naturalistic" presuppositions. Freud, the "father of modern psychology," offered some radical new ideas. He coined the terms and definitions of *id, ego,* and *superego.* Freud taught that man needed to be freed from his religious values and could find within himself all of the necessary guidelines to protect and advance society.

In fact, Freud went so far as to slander belief in God as a *mental disorder.* He taught that anyone who truly believed in God suffered from a deep-seated mental problem.

Freud tried to disassociate guilt from sin. Through psychoanalysis, he denied that there was a God anywhere to "trouble" man's mind or soul. Freud's psychoanalytical view of human beings has profoundly influenced Western thought.

Freud taught that man, his mind, and *his own* values are the ultimate basis for happiness and success, *without* any need for external or immutable divine laws. He believed that humans are essentially animals, driven by sexual impulses and instincts that are always in conflict with the standards of society.

Christopher Laudell, former dean of the Harvard Law School, expanded the radical thinking of Marx and Freud. According to his teachings, evolutionary principles must also be applied to judges' opinions. To him the U.S. Constitution is *relative,* changing, and should be *interpreted* by judges who could rule that law means whatever the judges want it to mean.

These men who were the radical thinkers of Europe and America during the last century were admired and followed by only a few. What united them in thought was the one thing they had in common: with the exception of Darwin, they were all atheists.

These intellectuals dismissed the idea of a supernatural Creator God. They rejected the idea of absolute laws or values and believed all standards were relative. They believed that *man without God* was the essence of life and that man was free to choose his own destiny, without being subject to God or His laws.

Soul Of Humanism

The source of personal presuppositions is of ultimate importance. If God is the source of our beliefs and values, our philosophy will be based on Godly absolutes and His ideals.

Whatever is *not* of God is a departure *from* God and from absolute Godly ideals. The *source* for that departure, or anti-God philosophy, is *man himself*.

Personal *philosophy* ("as a man thinketh") determines personal actions and politics ("so is he"). The culture that expresses a *God-centered* world view and lifestyle is expressing *Theism*.

MAN←	— SOURCE —	→ GOD
Relative←	— Beliefs —	→ Absolute
No Values←	— Values —	→ Ideals/Laws

When the source of a philosophy is the *mind of man*, its expression is *Humanism*. Critics of fundamental or evangelical Christians often take them to task for using this word "Humanism" without definition.

Humanism has been defined even by Humanists themselves as *against Theism*, as a repudiation of the beliefs and values of those who align themselves with God. Humanism is best comprehended when its relationship to Theism is understood.

Theism is the God-centered view of life that puts the Creator God as the source of all thought and actions. In the Old Testament, there is a pivotal passage (see chapter 6 of this book) that is called the Great Commandment. It teaches us to *"love* the Lord thy God with all thine heart . . . soul . . . might.''* It further commands us to "teach . . . thy children" to love and serve God.

In the New Testament, the pivotal passage is the Great Commission, which basically teaches the same thing but also includes teaching about the Atonement—a *positive* and *optimistic* response to the fall of man. God gives mankind the first reason for optimism by providing for man's redemption.

Historians tell us the greatest feature of early education was its *optimism*. Optimism played a major role in our nation's growth, development, and success. And where do we find optimism in our culture? The answer is in the Bible, the Atonement, and the Redemption of man. *Theism builds up*; it builds up the individual, the society, the nation, culture, and civilization.

The "soul" of Humanism is atheism, because Humanism depends on God's *non*existence. The word "atheist" comes from the Greek *atheos*, which means "without god." Because *atheist* has such negative connotations, many Humanists prefer to call themselves *non*-Theists instead of atheists. But the meaning is still the same. They reject the God of the Bible and therefore have no god.

Humanism is the man-centered life: man at his best or his worst—it doesn't matter. Man-centered Humanism has *no standards* beyond those man creates for himself. It focuses on man's own importance and achievements.

Humanism is *negative* and *pessimistic*. This man-centered philosophy and lifestyle *results in the progressive destruction of* the individual, the society, the nation, culture, and civilization. When we *systematically train a generation to think and reason everything from man's point of view,* where everything is chaotic and relative, and where there are no absolutes, we have no philosophical tools with which to *build up* a life or instill optimism into the culture. By the beginning of the twentieth century, atheistic Humanism became a growing intellectual force and influence.

State Control
As early as the 1870s, the removal of the Bible and religion from the curriculum of government schools had begun, and state control of education was born. By 1900 only ten percent of America's children were still enrolled in private or church-related schools. Public schools had taken ninety percent of the children.

But in the early 1900s the Bible was still on the desk of most teachers, and the principles of the Bible, including absolute values, still dominated the teaching curriculum. Biblical values were accepted as the prevailing cultural consensus.

When the consensus is attached to righteous values and beliefs, society reflects this in tranquility, order, morality, character, and stewardship. But when the consensus is led away from absolute principles, there is permissiveness, confusion, lawlessness, decline in morals and character, and poverty.

Our nation was built upon *Theism*—from the early 1600s until approximately 1900. Then a dramatic shift in cultural consensus, directed by an accumulation of Humanist influences, caused the most significant changes in the history of the world.

A new secular religion was moving to center-stage, while modern education was taking form. The roots of modern education, and of the crisis that it has spawned, had been established in the philosophical soil of America. The climate was ripe for a sweeping new ideological revolution.

THREE

HUMANIST REVOLUTION

During the late 1800s the seeds of Humanism were sown in the fields of science, government, philosophy, psychology, and economics. The seeds had sprouted but had not quite begun to grow.

The writings of the radical Humanist intellectuals mentioned in the last chapter would probably have collected dust on library shelves if it had not been for a man named John Dewey.

Atheistic Philosophy

In the 1920s Dewey, an eminent graduate professor at Columbia University in New York City, taught the relativist principles of modern Western philosophers.

Dewey was influenced by Fabian Socialists, a radical campus movement that later became known as Students for a Democratic Society. Their left-action view of a "democratic society" drew heavily from Robert Owen, Karl Marx, and G. W. F. Hegel. Their left-action groups produced the radical leaders of the 1950s and 1960s.

In his book *School and Society*, John Dewey asserted that there are *no unchanging truths* or *eternal principles*. Dewey wrote the following:

> There is no God and there is no soul. Hence, there are no needs for the props of traditional religion. With dogma and creed excluded, then immutable truth is also dead and buried. There is no room for fixed natural law or absolutes.

Dewey adapted the educational ideas of Robert Owen and Horace Mann and developed a permissive "progressivism," which caught the fancy of educators. Dewey embraced the new man-centered philosophy of Humanism and watched with satisfaction as it swept into America's educational institutions.

Meanwhile other "intellectuals" of the time gave voice to the Humanist faith. For example, Julian Huxley, a founder of the American Humanist Association, offered this definition:

> I use the word "Humanist" to mean someone who believes that man . . . is not

under the control or guidance of any supernatural being or beings, but has to rely on himself and his own power.

Humanist author Paul Kurtz wrote:

We can discover no divine purpose or providence for the human species . . . no deity will save us; we must save ourselves.

Another Humanist author, John Dunphy, envisioned a full-scale assault on the citadels of learning:

I am convinced that the battle for humankind's future must be waged and won in the public school classrooms by teachers who correctly perceive their role as the proselytizers of a new faith: a religion of humanity. . . . The classroom must and will become an arena of conflict between the old and the new—the rotting corpse of Christianity, together with its adjacent evils and misery, and the new faith of Humanism.

Charles Francis Potter wrote similarly:

Contemporary education is thus a most powerful ally of Humanism and every public school is a School of Humanism. What can a Theistic Sunday school, meeting for an hour once a week, reaching only a fraction of the children, do to stem the tide of a five-day program of Humanistic teaching?

Earlier Humanist writers and philosophers had laid the groundwork. In the area of politics, Friedrich Engels (1820-1895) had inspired Lenin, Stalin, and Mao Tse Tung to throw off religious superstition. Engels also inspired Hitler. Lenin, Stalin, Hitler, and Mao considered the ultimate ''solution'' to all economic, social, and religious problems to be the extermination of those who stood in the way of their ambitions.

Historians claim these few men were responsible for the deaths of over one hundred *million* people.

Marxist-Leninists believe that the end justifies any and all means. For the sake of the goal, it is permissible to lie, cheat, steal, and even kill others who stand in the way.

Hitler had his own brand of achievement by natural selection. He used evolutionary philosophy to promote his ideas of racial superiority.

Humanists would no doubt argue and disclaim any association between Humanist philosophy and the terror of Stalin and Hitler. But these men obviously took God out of the picture and became gods unto themselves and their people.

Communism is the supreme political expression of Humanism. It disregards God's law and governs by man's laws. "Thou shalt not kill" is replaced by "The end justifies the means."

Humanism began to affect U.S. society decisively when it swept into our educational system. What happened to Western culture and civilization was *not* an accident. There was a deliberately and carefully wrought revolution of Humanism.

It was a calculated plan to transform the culture and society significantly. This revolution was led by men who were rebels against their Creator and His laws. They were not all communists, but their objective was the same—abolition of God consciousness from American culture.

Godless Religion

Humanists at first declared themselves to be free of religion. But they had only separated themselves from God. They still *worshiped*—but now at the altar of man.

Is Humanism really a *religion?*

The *Humanist Manifesto* of 1933 expressed both a religious and a philosophical outlook. *On every page* the liberal Humanists who signed that historic document referred to themselves as "religious Humanists," or to their philosophy and beliefs as "religious Humanism."

In 1961 United States Supreme Court Justice

Stewart Potter declared Humanism to be, itself, a religion:

> Among religions in this country which do not teach what would generally be considered belief in the existence of God are Buddhism, Taoism, Ethical Culture, Secular Humanism and others.

When we talk about the Humanist revolution, we are really speaking about a new *religion* that replaces the God-centered life and system of beliefs. This religion would affect all areas of life and culture.

Is Humanism a religion? Psychologist Erich Fromme defines *religion* in these words:

> Any group-shared system of thought and action that offers the individual a frame of orientation and an object of devotion.

This "frame of orientation" or "devotion" involves a world view—a defined set of assumptions and presuppositions that originate with man instead of God.

The presuppositions of Humanist religion include these:

- There is no God.
- Life began by chance.

- Life developed through evolutionary processes.
- Moral standards are relative; permissiveness is good.
- The Bible is myth, superstition.
- Jesus Christ is not God, but just another man.

The Humanists have taken their "religion" seriously. As a result, the *American public school system is now completely governed by the Humanist religion.*

Transformed Society

The Western world had actually come to share the Humanist-communist-materialist vision. Secular man was caught up in the desire to embrace a world without God. But by denying God's existence, he also denied the reality of his own sin and guilt and their consequences. By exalting man to replace God, secular man stooped to the ultimate folly—the denial of accountability to God.

"The fool," said David, *"hath said in his heart, 'There is no God'"* (Ps. 14:1).

Neither individuals nor nations will be excused forever. People simply cannot rebel against God's principles without consequences.

The *Humanist Manifesto,* signed in 1933 by eleven prominent college and university professors and other liberals, espoused a new religion that was anti-God, anti-Bible, and anti-supernatural. It renounced traditional Biblical morality and standards. The Humanists declared themselves to be against the capitalist system and independent of Biblical absolutes. They were "bound" only by man's reason, values, and opinions.

That same year (1933) brought a wave of dominant Humanist influence into every major area of American life.

EDUCATION—John Dewey and others actively were shifting the system to the left in the name of "progressive" education and government consolidation.

LAW—The judicial system began to "interpret" the Constitution and declare that it "meant" what *they* decreed, in a move sharply away from absolutes.

GOVERNMENT—Bureaucrats pushed for more and more programs of social welfare, increased government spending, and limited private initiative.

ECONOMICS—The gold standard was abolished. People were beginning to be motivated by chaotic changing values, greed, and relativism; the entire system was undermined and unstable.

RELIGION—Humanist-modernist influence

invaded mainstream denominations. Radical, free-thinking intellectuals questioned traditional beliefs and doctrines, especially in Theological seminaries. As a result, growing numbers of clergymen were led away from Biblical faith and truth.

Western society had been effectively transformed. Humanistic presuppositions had replaced Theistic ones. The Theological roots of America had been severed. Humanism ruled.

A new day had dawned. It was the bright day of the shining city of man. Enthusiastic advocates envisioned the building of a great new society on new foundations. Surely, they speculated, something approaching millennial splendor would soon be ushered in through human effort.

But were these optimistic expectations to become a reality? We turn next to an examination of the program that emerged out of the Humanist obsession. As we shall see, the Humanist stranglehold on America was to result in devastating consequences.

HUMANIST PROGRAM

The Humanist program featured a bold, energetic, and pervasive onslaught against traditional American society and established values. The practice of praying in public schools was challenged. Textbooks were altered to ridicule Christianity while praising humanism. The foundation of church life and doctrine were undermined. Many campuses were subverted. Human life was degraded and the family was assaulted.

Prayer Prohibited
Humanists challenged traditional religious practices in the government schools, practices that were taken for granted by most Americans. Biblical principles, Bible reading, religious morality, and daily devotions were challenged under the

flimsy accusation that they constituted an *"estab-lishment* of religion" and were in violation of the First Amendment of the Constitution, which provides for the separation of Church and State.

On June 25, 1962, prayer recitations were banned. The Supreme Court, in a five-three decision, ruled that a twenty-two word "official prayer" in New York public schools was a violation of the First Amendment to the U.S. Constitution.

That simple prayer read as follows: *"Almighty God, we acknowledge our dependence on thee and beg thy blessing over us, our parents, our teachers, and our nation."* Next to go was Bible reading. Then, private prayer. These moves caught Christians by surprise.

Dr. Hubert P. Block was a minister and teacher in those days. He relates his experience:

> I was teaching in the public schools of St. Clair County, Alabama, in 1951. The public schools were so different at that time. The state of Alabama mandated by law that the Bible be read each morning and that each teacher should instruct on the evil effects of alcohol and tobacco. We also had prayer and sang spiritual hymns each day. Since I was a minister I was invited to speak at the school-wide chapel service which was conducted weekly.

Dr. Block adds that the parents were not at all upset by this. In fact, he says, ''The parents were delighted that their children had a Christian teacher.''

When Rev. Leonard Allgood came to Plano, Texas, in 1958, he was asked to take part in regular school chapel and devotional exercises. He says, ''Each morning for a week at a time we would read Scripture, comment on it, and have prayer.''

Rev. Allgood adds, ''This continued until the middle sixties, when we were no longer allowed to have morning devotions in the school.''

Textbooks Corrupted

During this period, in order to avoid controversy, school textbook publishers dropped all mention of Christianity. Only a small percentage of school districts in the entire country now offer even an elective course in religion. But even such ''religion-neutral'' courses put teachers and school officials on the defensive.

In *U.S. News & World Report* (7/4/88), writer Jill Rachlin reports: ''Religion has played a crucial role in shaping history, but you wouldn't know it from reading today's textbooks.''

Contemporary textbooks are biased against the traditional Judeo-Christian religious heritage. Pilgrims are *not* described as fleeing persecution to practice worship in freedom, which was the historic reason for their emigration to the New World.

The ''meaning'' of Thanksgiving is explained

simply as a day set aside by the pilgrims to *thank the Indians*; no reference is made to God or religion.

No mention of God is permitted, yet textbooks favorably discuss Secular Humanism, Buddhism and other Eastern religions, witchcraft, and the occult.

Textbooks, in general, deny the truth about the value and effect of Christianity by failing to report their impact on history—especially during periods of spiritual awakening when Christianity has contributed to national reform. Even the liberal lobby group, People for the American Way, admits that Christianity influences American culture.

U.S. News reports that a coalition of religious leaders and educators (Americans United Research Foundation) have joined to put religion back into the classroom. The group has published a pamphlet, "Religion in the Public School Curriculum" that suggests what schools may or may not do—according to the Constitution and in light of court rulings:

Public schools can teach *about* religion, providing:
- It is academic and not devotional.
- It explains the role of religion in history and civilization.
- It aims to make students aware of different religions without implied favoritism.
- It does not invoke religious authority to

teach moral values.

- It does not promote or denigrate any single religion.

While on the surface this may sound acceptable, it does not go far enough for Christians, who are concerned about several points:

- It leaves *God* out, and a "neutral" course on religion teaches no accountability.
- Without the teaching of the Atonement, there is no source of *optimism*.
- Without absolute principles there are no moral values, no sense of direction.
- It places the teacher in a position to *interpret*.
- The value of any course will depend on the life and world view (Humanist or Theist) of the teacher.

The fact is, without God a public school elective on "religion" remains a compromised position and a type of Humanism. It cannot build a base of character in youth.

Christianity Under Attack

Some years ago atheist Madalyn Murray O'Hair founded an organization of fellow atheists. This small minority, consisting of only about .00048 percent of the population at the time, was able to enlist the Supreme Court to move from a *neutral position* toward religion to an *anti-Christian position*.

This society of militant unbelievers stated that its primary objectives were to remove "In God We Trust" as our national motto and "under God" from the Pledge of Allegiance. They also wanted to ban prayers and religious holidays at *any public place*, to challenge the oath of office for the public officials ("so help me God"), and to eliminate tax benefits or exemptions for religious organizations.

Subsequently the Supreme Court of the United States struck down a Kentucky state law that required the posting of the Ten Commandments in schoolrooms. Their ruling stated that the Ten Commandments were "plainly religious," adding that they "may induce children to read, meditate upon, perhaps to venerate and to obey the commandments."

It is absolutely inconceivable that the Supreme Court would rule against the Ten Commandments on the basis that some child might be *induced to obey them*!

Prayer has been banned from American schools, God and religion erased from our history books, and observance of Christmas and Easter secularized. Public parks and city malls are no longer available for religious holiday displays or programs.

In New York City and other major cities, the law prohibits distribution of religious literature in public places.

Atlanta, Los Angeles, and a number of other cities have made it illegal to hold a Bible study or prayer meeting—even in a private home—without a permit from city officials. Zoning laws are used to stop or neutralize religious groups and churches. In Rockford, Illinois, a church group was told it could not use the building it bought for a Christian school. The building they purchased was *already* a school building, sold at surplus by the school board. Yet government officials declared the school illegal because of violation of zoning laws.

The communist and Humanist agendas agree. In both societies the practice of religious freedom is restricted or even forbidden. Religious symbols are frequently disallowed in public places.

Church Neutralized

In America, Humanists have found an effective means of neutralizing the Church: simply declare Christian beliefs to be political. Thus homosexuality, abortion, and similar issues are no longer religious matters but "human rights" or "political" issues.

When churches or religious groups act in a manner contrary to "public policy," such as opposition to homosexual "rights," abortion, or other politicized moral issues, they risk losing their tax-exempt status or otherwise jeopardize their religious freedoms.

Obviously, America's religious liberty is now all but eliminated. It may be too late to recover a national consensus of Theism.

But weren't we taught that America was established as a Christian nation? The U.S. Supreme Court said in 1878 that the legal structure of America is Christian in nature, and equated civilization with Judeo-Christian moral standards.

Even as recently as 1952 the Supreme Court said, "We are a religious people whose institutions presuppose a Supreme Being." Our founding fathers never suspected that the governmental, educational, and political organizations would someday become actively engaged in carrying out anti-Theistic policies.

Actually, by the time religion and prayer were banned from school by the Supreme Court, it didn't matter much. A neutralized church and religious complacency had already opened the door to Humanism. The Humanists in the educational system had practically achieved their goal *without* the Court's help.

In just one generation, the philosophy of Humanism expressed in Humanist *actions* had filtered down from the educational leaders to the people. American society had begun reaping the fruits of Humanism.

Campus Subverted

By the 1960s the philosophy of Humanism had permeated the college and university campuses. And it brought utter chaos—from Columbia University on the East Coast, to Kent State in the Midwest, to Berkeley on the West Coast. To say that social change was occurring would be to understate the situation.

Revolution was taking place. Rebellion against laws, rules, and order was the "in thing" at the university level in the 1960s. By the end of that decade, campus anarchy had filtered down to the high school level. By the early 1970s student rebellion was spreading through the junior high schools, and by the end of the 1970s it had become an elementary school problem.

While much of the anarchy and rebellion was loosely aimed at unsettling the *status quo* of society, some used the times to demonstrate for certain "rights" and against perceived inequities.

Human Life Degraded

By 1973 homosexual groups were demanding employment and housing "rights" and political recognition. And women were seeking the "right" to abort pregnancies. Soon there were children's "rights" supporters, drug-use advocates, and those who wanted the "right" to disobey draft laws or other legislation that they regarded as disagreeable.

The 1960s and 1970s were years in which just about anyone could (and nearly everyone did!) demand some kind of "rights." Some causes were just and noble; others were frivolous. Some even set dangerous precedents.

A consistent Biblical principle insists that rights must be accompanied with equal levels of responsibility. But without the influence of Biblical morality and traditional values, minority "rights" were demanded (and given) at the cost of *majority* rights.

And who defended the rights of the unborn when women claimed the "right" to abort their babies?

Humanist Manifesto II was signed in 1973. Like its predecessor, which had been signed forty years earlier, it was designed to promote Humanist aims and causes. However, *Humanist Manifesto II* was even more blatant and aggressively anti-Christian. It was endorsed by vast numbers of organizations as well as by a great host of influential individuals—entertainers, politicians, educators, scientists, and representatives from nearly every discipline: law, medicine, religion, the military, business, and communications.

That same year (1973), a woman sued the state of Texas. "Jane Roe" said she had been raped, and she sought to terminate the resulting pregnancy by abortion.

The case, *Roe vs. Wade*, went all the way to the Supreme Court. The following statement is the crucial portion of Justice Harry A. Blackmun's majority ruling:

> A fetus is not a person under the Constitution and thus had no legal right to life.

That statement means a woman's ("pro-choice") decision to abort her unborn child is a "right" she may enjoy because under the constitutional law, the baby has *no right to live*.

So, in 1973 the Supreme Court decreed that the laws of all fifty states were wrong. It legalized abortion and neutralized the existing moral codes based upon Biblical principles, which held abortion to be the same as murder.

On what basis did the jurists decide? Nothing in the Constitution addressed the issue. But as previously pointed out, Humanism declares that the law (even the Constitution) says *what we want it to say*.

Adolf Hitler also used this strategy to redefine "personhood." Hitler altered the laws to decree that Jews and other minorities were "non-persons." At the war crimes trials following World War II, Nazis argued that they broke no laws. They had slaughtered millions of Jews and others but had done so with the sanction of German law. In the same way, the Supreme Court declared unborn children to be "nonpersons."

A horrible "holocaust" of *over one million* abortions are now performed every year. Since abortion was legalized, many *millions of lives* have been ended by this cruel and immoral practice, sacrificed at the altar of complacency and Humanistic expediency.

In 1988 "Jane Roe" admitted that she had lied about being raped. In reality she had become pregnant by an estranged lover, and she had invented the story about being raped. The historic court case, which unleashed the ongoing holocaust of abortion deaths, was based upon a hoax!

How far the courts have come from Biblical morality and principles!

In the Bible there is an illustration of what God thinks about the value of life—even an unborn child:

> If men strive, and hurt a woman with child, so that her fruit depart from her, and yet no mischief follow: he shall be surely punished, according as the woman's husband will lay upon him; and he shall pay as the judges determine. And if any mischief follow, then thou shalt give life for life, eye for eye, tooth for tooth, hand for hand, foot for foot, burning for burning, wound for wound, stripe for stripe (Exod. 21:22-25).

To illustrate this passage, let's suppose a man gets into an argument with his neighbor. The argument becomes heated, and the two men resort to physical force. Then the neighbor's pregnant wife runs over in defense of her husband. In the struggle the other man pushes her away. She falls to the ground. The incident brings on early labor, and the woman delivers.

Now, if "no mischief follow," apparently the baby lives. However, the man who pushed her is still punished. The husband can exact a punishment of his own choosing and can demand money as reparations, to be determined by a judge.

However, if "mischief follows" (which supposes the baby dies) then "thou shalt give life for life." In God's eyes, the life of an unborn child has the same value as the life of a full-grown man. God confers "person" status to a fetus and guarantees its *legal* right to life according to Holy Scripture. But man's law (unholy Humanism) says the unborn has "no legal right to life."

Family Assaulted

Legalized abortion is only one example of how the *fruits of Humanism* have had an impact on Western culture.

Next, the religion of Secular Humanism, through its followers in the courts and government agencies, began to attack other structures of Theism—especially the family.

God created the family as a model unit for society. It is within the family that a person learns about God, esteem for others, love, self-control, and service.

The family is the unique, powerful agent for producing the Christian faith in succeeding generations. So it is no wonder that those whose aim is to destroy Christianity would be moved to neutralize or eradicate the traditional family structure. The objective was to destroy the family and capture the child.

Bills were introduced in the early 1970s to make the government a "partner" with parents in child-rearing. *Children's rights* were declared to need governmental supervision.

Both the religion of Secular Humanism and socialist philosophy contend that the child is the *property* of the state and doesn't really belong to his parents or to God. Nazi philosophy agrees.

Theoretically, if parents and children are in conflict, the government can step in on behalf of the child. In effect, this action supersedes the divinely established authority of parents.

In practice, various state agencies (such as welfare and health departments) have already tested the system.

Parents have been arrested and jailed for "child abuse" after spanking their children.

In 1987 two representatives from a child welfare agency came to a minister's home after someone reported hearing him say in a sermon that he advocated spanking as a form of child discipline. The welfare people decided the pastor and his wife were unfit parents because they admitted to spanking their children. They presented the couple with a demand that called for compliance with five orders:

1. The parents must no longer use corporeal punishment to discipline their children.
2. The pastor and his wife must permit the welfare agency to come at any time to visit the home. They visit twice weekly to ''inspect'' the children for bruises.
3. The pastor and his wife must accept agency supervision.
4. The entire family is subject to psychiatric assessment.
5. The pastor is forbidden to leave town without first checking with the welfare agency.

If the minister does not comply or spanks his children in defiance of welfare department orders, he will be in jeopardy of serving time in jail and having his children taken away from him, all without a trial. He says, ''My name has been added to the Child Abuse Registry . . . and I haven't even been convicted in court.'' Now, whose ''rights'' are being violated?

Welfare agencies, educational bureaucracies, licensing and zoning boards, and tax agencies, along with numerous other government agencies, are acting in the same arrogant manner. Their rulings have *the force of law* beyond the scope of legislation. They can arbitrarily question and *deny Christian rights* under the Constitution *without due process* and *despite the fact that Christians are breaking no laws*!

By the end of the 1960s the Humanist program had taken root and was running rampant through the entire fabric of American society. It is an unfailing axiom of history that any movement will inevitably become known by its fruits. We turn next to an examination of some of the more obvious fruits of the Humanist program as demonstrated in our society.

F I V E

FRUITS OF HUMANISM

The fruits of Humanist ideology and programming in American life have become increasingly obvious with the passage of time. Among the more prominent of these fruits have been the mass introduction of evolutionary propaganda, the virtual exclusion of parents from the educational process, a crisis of academic failure, a deteriorating value system, counter-productive sex education, child abuse in the schools, moral decay, social violence, a holocaust of disease, and cultic delusions of the "new age."

Evolutionary Propaganda

A research team from Richardson, Texas, called *Foundation for Thought and Ethics*, published a poll conducted by *Austin Analytical Consulting*. Dan Austin, who heads the firm, holds a Ph.D. degree in anthropology and has five years' experience teaching Ph.D.-level anthropology at Southern Methodist University.

The poll asked biology teachers nationwide about their personal views of how living things began. Of those responding, 11.5 percent believed various life forms were created. The other 88.5 percent believed life began by some form of evolutionary process.

Both ideas are *theories*. No human who lives on Earth today was around when life began, so it's impossible to *prove* through purely scientific procedures whether life was created or simply evolved.

In 1981 the people of Arkansas took the usual, proper legislative steps through their elected representatives to correct what they felt was an unequal situation. The Humanist academic consensus had determined that only the evolutionary world-view theory of origins would be taught in the schools.

Parents and a group of educators sought to introduce what was called a *balanced treatment law*. This bill would require at least a balanced presentation of both creationist and evolutionist views of origins.

The bill, called *"An Act: Balanced Treatment for Creation Science and Evolution Science,"* was passed by state legislators and signed into law by the governor.

The ACLU then led an attack against the law. Despite the fact that the law represented the wishes of the majority of citizens through their elected representatives, the ACLU took the matter to court—and won. Understand that the people of Arkansas were not asking that Darwinian evolution be thrown out—simply that a balanced treatment include a creation viewpoint. That is what the courts threw out.

Judge William Overton struck down the Arkansas law, and the Arkansas Supreme Court upheld his ruling.

In Louisiana similar efforts to present a balanced viewpoint of origins were also defeated.

Today it is important to understand this point mandated by the courts and the ACLU:

> In American education, the science fiction of Darwin is the *only acceptable truth* for the scientific origins of the universe.

Secular Humanism is a willful, arrogant system that enjoys a controlled monopoly of government schools. It is not happening *just* in America but in all of Western civilization.

America and all Western nations are now reaping the harvest of that system. It is a harvest of shame, ruinous neglect, and increasing decadence.

Exclusion Of Parents

The reader may ask, ''Are you *against* the *public schools?''*

My answer is, "We *do not have* public schools. We have *government* schools. . . and one characteristic of them is that they largely exclude parents from the educational process.

There are three kinds of schools: *private, public* and *government*.

Private schools . . . are controlled directly by parents, who are actively involved in the entire educational process. They hire teachers (through *elected* administrators) and fund the educational process (usually through tuition). If these parents do not like the kind of schools, teachers, or curriculum they are paying for, they get together, vote to change, and act upon their choices or switch schools.

Public schools . . . are similar to private schools in that the parents control the educational process through a locally-elected representative body. They are financed collectively through local taxation. The teachers are hired and are subject to the elected administrator. If the schools or teachers do not measure up to the standards of the local parents' wishes, changes are made so that the schools *do* reflect the local mandate.

Government schools . . . are entirely different from both of the above models in that the *parents have no voice* in the educational process. They have no say in the financing, control, selection of textbooks or curriculum materials, or the hiring of teachers. The government educational agency operates the schools from local, state, and federal funds. "Educrats" are *appointed* and are *not* responsible to the parents. The main presupposition of government education is that *all children are the property and responsibility of the state.*

There is an accelerating trend in the United States toward the growth of government education. Many good people—parents concerned about their children's education and teachers who are committed to helping these children learn—are doing their best, but are unable to prevail against the basic Humanistic premises and philosophies of government schools. For this reason, many are placing their children in private schools.

Crisis Of Failure

A U.S. presidential commission found that government school systems are *failing miserably.* This failure is affecting whole generations of an entire culture. It is one of the destructive fruits of Humanism.

Teachers are leaving the government school system. Every year more and more of them abandon education like a crew leaving a sinking ship. They are going into private education or into business and industry.

According to *U.S. News & World Report* (5/26/86) one-fourth of all government schoolteachers say they are likely to quit teaching in the next five years. One-half of these teachers admit that if they had an opportunity to turn the clock back and select a vocation again, they would not choose teaching.

The government schools are many thousands of teachers short of their staff needs each year. As a result, qualification standards have been *lowered* to attract prospective teachers into the profession. Currently, high school graduates who choose teaching as a career score some *seventy points below the national average,* an average *two hundred points below* English and math majors.

This news dismays even the government school administrators themselves. Writer Sue Blumenthal, in *Leadership News* (4/15/88), a publication of the American Association of School Administrators, says, ''The NSTA estimates that a third of the nation's science classes are taught by unqualified teachers.''

What do the teachers themselves think about the quality of government education? Statistics show that twenty-seven percent, more than one-fourth of all teachers who teach in government schools, send *their* children to *private schools*—for the most part, *Christian* schools.

It is practically impossible for American parents to have confidence in U.S. school systems that are presenting a world view that is anti-family, anti-religious, and even anti-American.

The entire government educational system of the U.S.—from college and university level to high schools, to elementary school levels—is *flooded* with

Humanist-inspired attacks on traditional Western values. Some are subtle introductions of leftist, immoral, or anti-Christian philosophies; others are more obvious, such as immoral or incompetent teachers. All are eroding away any possible education from a Theistic and moral point of view.

For the past twenty-five years, academic achievement test scores have been on a steady decline. The real proof is in the students' scores on national tests such as the California Achievement Test. The CAT has *declined in difficulty* with each new edition.

When *U.S. News & World Report* asked twenty-two education experts to rate the elementary and secondary educational systems in various countries, America fared badly: "The U.S. finished fourteenth among the fifteen countries, just ahead of Thailand, just behind Hungary. Japan and West Germany scored best." Other studies show disappointing results—or worse.

One comparison showed that less than twenty-five percent of U.S. eleventh graders meet any minimum standards of competency in business, education, or the professions.

A test of American twelve-year-olds shows that twenty percent were unable to find their own country on a globe or world map.

U.S.A. Today (8/10/88) reports, "It's been said that if businesses were turning out the same quality of products as the schools, they would go bankrupt."

SAT Total Scores
1951 - 1986

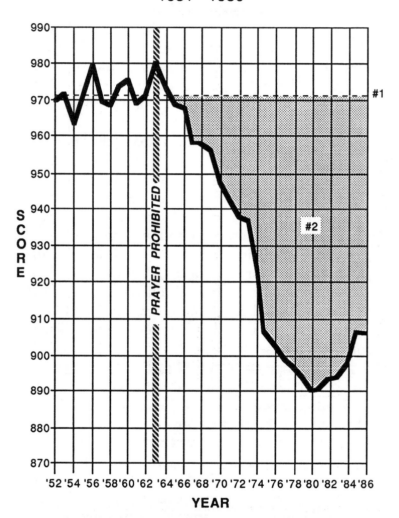

#1 - Average achievement level prior to the removal of prayer.

#2 - Amount of reduced academic achievement since the removal of prayer.

Basic data from the College Entrance Exam Board.

School Dropouts as Related To G.E.D. Testing 1949 - 1986

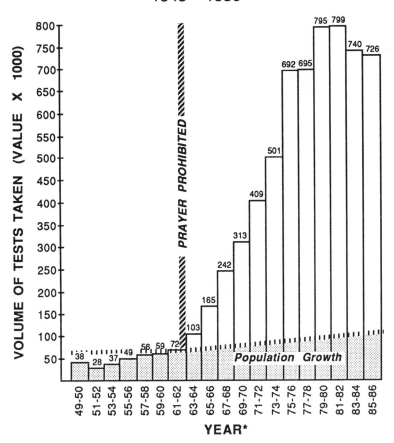

ιιιιιιιιιι Indicates population growth profile for subject age group.

* Groupings represent average tests taken per year for the two-year period.

Note: Since 1962 there have been 11 individual years in which the total students tested for that year surpassed the total of the 14 years prior to 1962.

Basic data from the General Educational Development Testing Service of The American Council on Education, *The 1986 GED Statistical Report,* and the Department of Commerce, Census Bureau.

At three thousand school dropouts a day across America, the *country* has over half a million dropouts every year.

According to a study done by the Education Commission of the States, U.S. adult illiteracy grows 1.5 million every year. One in ten of all Americans is illiterate and another forty million are only "marginally capable of exercising basic skills." As a result,

- Illiterate parents can't help their children in school.
- Billions of dollars are lost through low productivity, errors, and people on public assistance or welfare.
- Crime increases, as twenty percent of prison inmates are illiterate.

Despite the glut of billboards, brochures, pamphlets, radio and TV spots, marketing programs, and public relations campaigns promoting it, the Humanistic government school system is a failed one. And it is perpetuating its failure in the lives of the students, the real ones at risk.

Bankrupt Value System

Humanist beliefs destroy a child's sense of responsibility to God and the entire system of God-given authority. Humanist thought has produced pessimism, despair, and failure in the academic world. Ultimately it will spoil the minds of our children, and we will lose them. They will be sacrificed on the altar of anti-Christian propaganda.

> Beware lest any man spoil you through philosophy and vain deceit, after the tradition of men, after the rudiments of the world, and not after Christ (Col. 2:8).

"After the tradition of men" defines exactly the religion of Humanism.

The Humanist bureaucrats who have taken control of the American school system are building their program on the basis of assumptions that are assaulting our value system:

1. The school is the property of the state (government).
2. The child is the property of the state.
3. Those in charge and approved by the government can use the school to impose their own values on society.

Ironically, those in charge can change a Godly society into an immoral one "after the rudiments of the world" even without revolutionary force or the violent overthrow of government.

The government school, without parental

consent—and often without even parental knowledge—assumes unprecedented authority to

1. define the character and objectives of education,
2. prescribe curriculum and textbooks,
3. determine the qualifications of teachers and administrators,
4. determine, by certification or license, who can teach,
5. coerce, by compulsory education laws, children to attend government schools, and
6. prosecute parents and institutions, including churches, that do not cooperate with this authority.

Government education is pushing a bankrupt value system on America's children, and is usurping authority to force that system on parents and the entire nation.

Sex Education
Widespread sexual experimentation and permissiveness has resulted from the Humanist curriculum. Groups such as SIECUS (in the 1970s) and Planned Parenthood (in the 1980s) have made significant contributions to curriculum design.

Planned Parenthood also contributes Humanist principles to school curriculum and has established hundreds of clinics for dispensing birth control information, contraceptives, and family-planning advice. These clinics, supposedly for adults, are funded with over $30 million (annually) of tax dollars to teach the Humanist philosophy of "how to have your cake and eat it too." If the birth control pills or devices do not work, Planned Parenthood promotes many of the 400,000 abortions performed on teen-age girls every year.

In addition to Planned Parenthood, there are other clinics—many in the schools themselves—that dispense condoms and birth control pills, prescribe other contraceptives, and provide "family-planning" counseling for students. The first of such clinics opened in 1973, but it was generally opposed by parents' groups. But the "sex clinics" have emerged again, and are spreading across the country.

Sex education has always been controversial, so the subject is often given another title, with a vague course description, such as "Growth and Maturity," presented without "outside parental meddling."

The Daily Breeze (Torrance, CA, 5/4/86) bore this headline on the front page: "Talking About Sex: A New Candor At School."

After roll call, health teacher Patty Hedstrom told a class at Newton Middle

School in Torrance to sit in a circle. It was time to talk about sex. ''Remember what the pituitary glands do?'' Hedstrom asked the eleven and twelve year-olds, as she pointed to a chalkboard drawing.

''It sends hormones down to your sex glands,'' one boy said.

''That's right. Very good.'' she said, continuing with the lesson. Then she began reviewing male reproductive organs with the sixth grade class.

The vast majority of teachers are giving students a thorough and explicit sex education unlike their parents ever had.

The New American (1/19/87) commented on the article:

American school children can barely write ''at a minimal level.'' Numerous other studies have documented the scandalous decline in literacy, math, science, and virtually every other academic area; but parents can take comfort in the knowledge that little Johnny and Suzie are ''nearly experts on the subject of sexual reproduction.''

Twelve-year-old students, with boys and girls together, are shown films of erections and other "technical" aspects of intercourse. Most parents do not know what is taught or how it is presented.

In virtually every lesson on sex education, the student is left with the feeling that sex before marriage is all right, that homosexuality is perfectly natural and normal, and that those who think differently are somehow strange.

Curiously, scholastic standards have fallen during the past twenty years while sex education has become more explicit, perverse, and universal. Not only is premarital sex permitted and encouraged, but other sexual proclivities such as homosexuality and group sex are discussed in a "morally neutral" setting.

The New American (1/19/87) reports on the testimony of a Seattle-area housewife and mother, Mrs. Janet Brossard, who for three weeks sat in on her daughter's sex education classes:

> As part of her testimony, Mrs. Brossard presented a questionnaire that was given to 13-year-olds in the eighth grade:
>
> "Adolescent sexual behavior instructions: Indicate in the space provided the minimum age at which each of the behaviors listed is considered appropriate or acceptable in your value system. In other words, when is it okay to engage in _____?"

The child is then supposed to fill in the age for 25 activities: holding hands, kissing, French kissing, petting, masturbating, love-making with persons of the same sex, smoking marijuana, drinking booze, having intercourse, having a variety of sexual partners, living together, taking birth control pills, etc.

The obvious message sent to these youngsters is that all of these activities are fine; they need only determine for themselves the appropriate age at which to commence.

Child Abuse

In 1984, the U.S. Department of Education conducted hearings in seven key cities to help explain why Americans are so dissatisfied with government schools. Hundreds of parents participated.

The seven days of hearings produced over 1,300 pages of testimony. Mrs. Phyllis Schlafly, a national pro-family activist and author, acted as editor to put the testimony into readable form. These excerpts from the official transcript of the hearings were published in 1984 as a book titled *Child Abuse in The Classroom* (Crossway Books).

Witnesses at these hearings complained about socialist models and language, immoral brainwashing, sex education contrary to parental standards, situational ethics, and classroom courses that confused children about life, especially in making behavioral and moral choices.

The participating parents represented no single religious or political point of view. They included Protestants, Catholics, Mormons, and others. What brought them together was their mutual concern about what their children were being taught in government schools.

These examples, excerpted from the testimonies, (detailed in *Child Abuse In The Classroom*) reflect this concern, and their genuine anger:

EXAMPLE: Students were told by their teacher, "If your parents told you there is a God . . . they were lying to you."

EXAMPLE: *Life and Health,* a ninth grade textbook, says, "There are many options of sexual behavior: masturbation, petting, cunnilingus, fellatio, and intercourse. Also there are "other partner preferences . . . including homosexuality and bisexuality."

EXAMPLE: *English Journal* carried a recommendation that high school English teachers suggest homosexual literature for students.

EXAMPLE: Homosexuality was presented as an alternative lifestyle to fifth grade health classes.

EXAMPLE: Students are told, "Your parents' values are different from yours," and "Students are smart enough to make all their own decisions."

EXAMPLE: Neither marriage nor chastity are mentioned as options in whether to become sexually active. The text materials use labels and emotionally loaded terminology to convince youngsters that choices between marriage and chastity are really not appropriate. The textbook defines chastity as "old-fashioned" in its description of contemporary sexual standards.

EXAMPLE: Students are asked to write suicide notes and discuss death, write about their own drug use, betray parental privacy about jobs, religion, income, and other privileged information.

Parents who testified at those Department of Education hearings were justifiably concerned about school courses and textbooks. *Are you really aware of what your children are being taught in school?*

Many school textbooks teach immoral sexual standards, encourage drug use, approve of pornography, encourage Marxist-socialist models, and teach a philosophy of values based on each student's idea of what is acceptable. No objective standards of right and wrong are conveyed.

Moral Decay
Clearly a new cultural consensus came to replace Biblical morality and traditional values. Humanism expressed itself in the "new morality," and this increasingly wrought havoc on society

with the passage of time.

Future generations became disposable, as *Roe vs. Wade* made it easy, as well as legal, to kill unborn, unwanted children.

Marriage became something to be disposed of, if considered convenient. So, also, did the children of divorce. Fathers (and mothers!) simply walked away from their responsibilities as parents, and a new class of poor was created: young mothers with children whose husbands and fathers chose to ignore their alimony and child support obligations.

Women abandoned the traditional concepts of self-worth. They became equal partners in the sexual revolution. There were no more double standards. Women became as sexually permissive as men were perceived to be.

With the sexual revolution came pornography. Not just the so-called "soft-core porn" of slick color magazines with subdued, air-brushed photography, but graphic, grisly, violent pornography and even "kiddie porn."

The self-destructive "disposable" ethic also demonstrated itself in drugs. The "flower children" glorified drug experimentation, and pot smoking became so acceptable that "everybody" was doing it. Pot smoking spread to the military in Vietnam, to colleges and business schools—even law schools where at least one Supreme Court nominee tried it.

Anti-pornography laws were loosened across

America. Smut exploded; so did prostitution and homosexuality. Times Square and Hollywood Boulevard were no longer tourist attractions for the mainstream. They became cluttered, as did districts in thousands of other towns in America, with sleazy smut stores, adult theaters, porn shops, massage parlors, and prostitutes. These hard-core perversions attracted drug addicts, criminals and teen-age runaways. Youngsters as young as ten sold themselves as prostitutes.

Pornography, witchcraft, Satan worship, and sexual immorality are now as widespread as pot and cocaine abuse. Pornography and violence are widely distributed as "entertainment" in slick, colorful packages—in films, videos, magazines, TV shows, and music—and brought into millions of homes.

Abortions are epidemic. Illegitimate birth rates have skyrocketed. X-rated rock music, crime, and occult religions are no longer practiced by just the counter-culture. The Humanist revolution has brought them to a greater or lesser degree into virtually every school and living room.

David Barton is the author of a carefully researched 1988 study titled *America: To Pray or Not To Pray* (P.O. Box 397; Aledo, TX 76008). Barton's book is based on the thesis that some remarkable things have happened as a result of a Supreme Court ruling. He writes, " . . . on June 25, 1962, 39 million students were told they could no longer do what they and their predecessors had been doing for years—pray in school."

In the famous *Engel vs. Vitale* case, the Supreme Court effectively banned school prayer. Barton's book documents and illustrates with a series of graphs how massive cultural change followed that decision to remove the acknowledgement of God and how that change has been to America's detriment.

With author David Barton's permission, we have reproduced twelve illustration plates from his book. Nine of the graphs are inserted to amplify this subheaded section titled "Moral Decay" (pages 84-90) and the section titled "Violent Times" (pages 93,94). Two were inserted previously in this chapter under the subhead "Crisis of Failure" (pages 70,71). And one is used to augment the material in the section titled "Disease Holocaust" (page 100).

Please note carefully each of the plates and view the trends in the context of the period following 1962.

As you will see, the resulting cultural change of the past twenty-five years is startling.

Pre-Marital Sex

Percentage of U.S. Teenage Women
Who Have Had Pre-Marital Intercourse

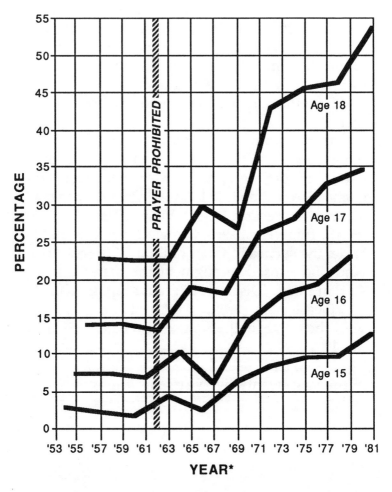

* Information was available in three (3) year groupings only.

Basic data from *Family Planning Perspectives,* Vol. 19, No. 2, March/April 1987.
Furnished by the Alan Guttmacher Institute.

Pregnancies To Unwed Women
Under 15 Years of Age

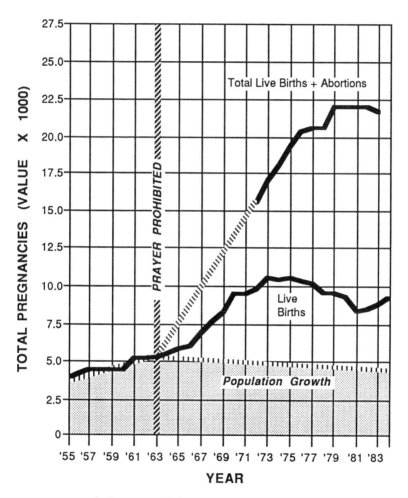

IIIIIIIIIII Indicates population growth profile for subject age group.
ᴧᴧᴧᴧᴧᴧᴧᴧᴧᴧ Indicates extrapolated data.

Basic data from Department of Health and Human Services, *Statistical Abstracts of the United States*, the Center for Disease Control, and the Department of Commerce, Census Bureau.

Pregnancies To Unwed Women
15-19 Yrs. Of Age

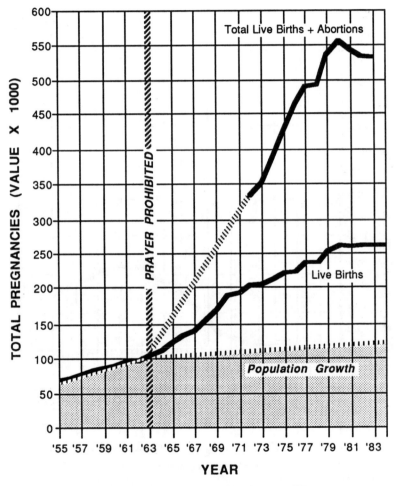

IIIIIIIIIII Indicates population growth profile for subject age group.

⁁⁁⁁⁁⁁⁁⁁⁁⁁⁁ Indicates extrapolated data.

Basic data from Department of Health and Human Services, *Statistical Abstracts of the United States,* the Center for Disease Control, and the Department of Commerce, Census Bureau.

Unmarried Couples

A Man and a Woman Who Live Together

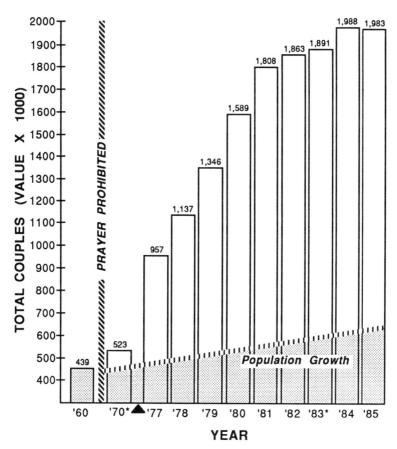

▲ Prior to 1977, unmarried couples living together was such a small group that data on this group was collected only in the 10-year census reports.

* Note: Unmarried couples represented only 1 in 85 of all couples in 1970, compared with 1 in 25 in 1983.

Basic data from "Marital Status and Living Arrangements: March 1985," Current Population Reports, Population Characteristics, Series P-20, No. 410; U.S. Department of Commerce, Bureau of the Census.

Divorce Rates

Divorces Per 1,000 Total Population

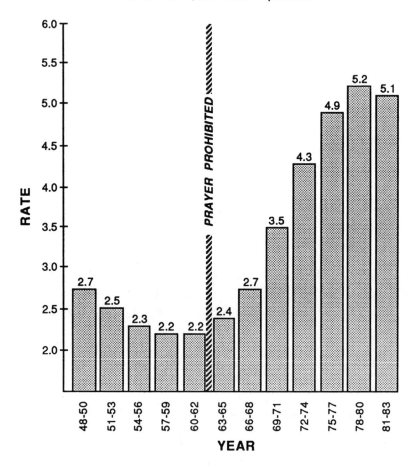

RATE

YEAR

PRAYER PROHIBITED

Notes: "The U.S. is at the top of the world's divorce charts on marital breakups." *U.S. News and World Report,* June 8, 1987, pgs. 68-69.

"The number of divorces tripled each year between 1962 and 1981." *Time,* July 13, 1987, pg. 21.

Basic data from the Department of Health and Human Services, *Monthly Vital Statistics Report,* Sept. 25, 1986.

Single Parent Households
1951 - 1985

Female Head, No Spouse Present

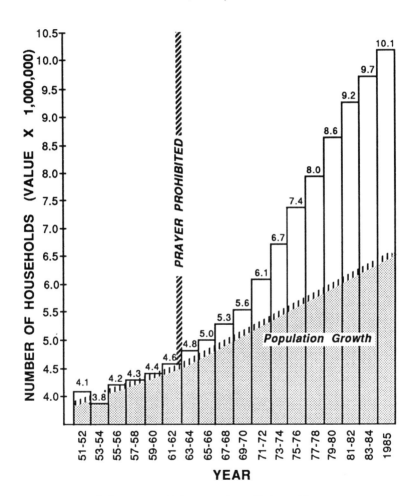

IIIIIIIII Indicates population growth profile for subject age group.

Basic data from *Statistical Abstracts of the United States,* and the Deparment of Commerce, Census Bureau.

Alcohol Consumption
Per Capita

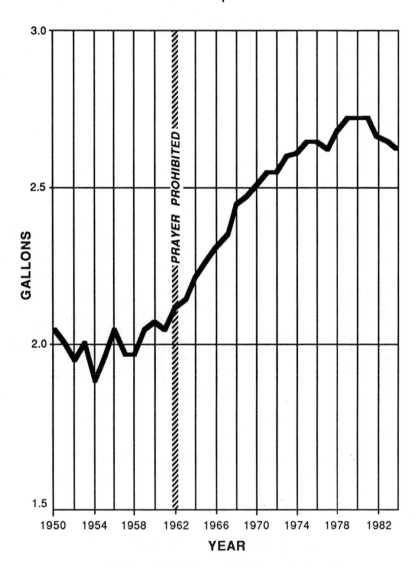

Basic data from National Clearinghouse for Alcohol Consumption.

Violent Times

When the "morally neutral" curriculum is taught for the most part by Humanists with relative values or none at all, the results are predictable.

- One-fifth of all teens have a drinking problem.
- Twenty to thirty percent of ninth graders entering high school do not graduate (fifty to sixty percent in inner-city schools).
- Fifty-six percent of teen-age girls and thirty-five percent of teen boys report that it is hard to cope with stress at home and school.
- Suicide is epidemic:

  ...Forty-two percent of all teen-age girls give "serious thought" to suicide.

  ...One-fourth of the boys also think about killing themselves.

  ...One in five girls will actually attempt suicide, and ten percent of all boys will try to kill themselves.
- Drug abuse is everywhere, even in the schools:

  ...One in ten eighth and tenth grade students smoke pot.

  ...One in fifteen adolescents uses cocaine.
- Sex and violence are growing patterns:

...One in five girls reports someone tried to *force* her to have sex.

...400,000 teen abortions occur yearly.

...Two and one-half million teens are infected with sexually transmitted diseases every year.

...Of the one million runaways and six million homeless children, many of them end up as male and female prostitutes on the streets.

In Chicago over 120 gangs intimidate students and teachers, peddle drugs, and create violence.

Over $600 million each year is spent by schools to fix or replace vandalized or stolen school property.

Juveniles now commit thirty-four percent of the violent crime, and as much as half of all crime, in America.

Youths, themselves, are more likely than other age groups to be victims of school and street crime.

Each year there are over three million incidents of attempted or completed assaults, rapes, robberies, and thefts in schools or on campuses.

One out of eighteen youths is assaulted, raped, or robbed annually.

The arrest rate for youths (ten to seventeen) just about *tripled* from 1960 to the mid-1970s, and by 1986 was ten times higher than in 1960.

Violent Crime:
Number Of Offenses

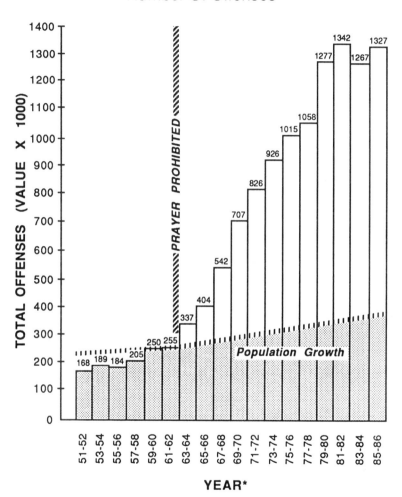

IIIIIIIIII Indicates population growth profile for subject age group.

* Groupings represent average rate per year over the two-year period.

Basic data from *Statistical Abstracts of the United States,*
and the Department of Commerce, Census Bureau.

Suicide Rates
Ages 15 - 24

Suicides Per 100,000 Total Population

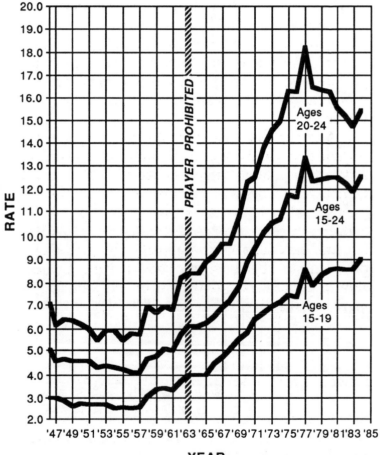

Basic data from National Center for Health Statistics, based on published and
unpublished statistical data, Division of Vital Statistics, Department of Health
and Human Services.

Juvenile arrests for serious crimes, according to the FBI, account for almost a third (thirty percent) of all arrests. However, juveniles make up only twenty percent of the overall population.

Surprisingly, the biggest increase in violent crime is not from poor, nonwhite neighborhoods. Overall, violent delinquency increased eighty-six percent among nonwhites, but five hundred percent among whites, many from affluent neighborhoods.

Another vice that has captured teen-agers is compulsive gambling. According to a survey of 2,700 high school students, about half of them gamble at least once a year. Thirteen percent finance their gambling with crimes. Five percent are pathological gamblers, as compared with only 1.5 percent of gambling adults who are classified as "pathological." Criminal behaviors motivated by the compulsion to gamble include theft of money, embezzlement, and armed robberies (*U.S. News & World Report*; 6/18/90).

A number of publications have illustrated the vast social changes by contrasting the "rules of conduct" for school children, "then and now."

The following list was compiled by the Fullerton, California, Police Department, the California Department of Education, and the Bristol, Virginia, *Herald Courier* (4/20/87):

MOST FREQUENT SCHOOL PROBLEMS
In the 1940s

- Excessive talking
- Chewing gum
- Making noise
- Running in the halls
- Getting out of turn in line
- Wearing improper clothing
- Not putting paper in wastebasket

In the 1980s

- Drug abuse
- Alcohol abuse
- Pregnancy
- Suicide
- Rape
- Robbery
- Assault
- Burglary
- Arson
- Bombings
- Murder
- Absenteeism
- Vandalism
- Extortion
- Gang warfare
- Abortion
- Venereal disease

In the old West, Jesse James, Billy the Kid, and other "outlaws"—although highly glamorized in books and movies—were nevertheless an exception to the rule. Gunfights, even in the streets of the old West, were actually rare incidents.

Today, a century later, that is no longer the case. *Newsweek* (1/11/88) reported the following:

> Gunfights are replacing fistfights as firearms become a major problem in the nation's schools.

> All across America, the number of children using and being harmed by guns is rising at an alarming rate. According to the U.S. Department of Justice, more than 27,000 youths between 12 and 15 were handgun victims. . . . But officials admit that as grim as those statistics are, they grossly understate the extent of the problem.

> Youth gangs in Los Angeles protect their turf with black-market U2 submachine guns and Russian-made AK-47 assault rifles.

> Nowhere is the proliferation of firearms among our youth more startling than in city high schools. . . . Hallway disputes that were once settled with fists or the

flashing of a knife blade end in a burst of firepower and a bloody corpse. Currently the total number of murders in the U.S.A. is approximately 25,000 annually.

Disease Holocaust

The fruits of Humanism have been unmistakable—an epidemic of crime, abortion, drug abuse, Satanism, occultism, child abuse, pornography, alcoholism, atheism, sexual immorality, and homosexuality. These came about through a *conditioning process*. This conditioning began with Humanist educators who propagated the idea that immoral actions were not wrong, merely "different" personal preferences.

By the late 1970s the "sex revolution" had done more than promote promiscuity. An article in *Time* told about a new epidemic—*genital herpes*.

Herpes is a sexually transmitted disease that became a badge of the sexually liberated "flower children."

Modern science even came to the aid of "sexually active" (a new euphemism for *promiscuous*) men, women, and growing numbers of teen-agers. Syphilis and gonorrhea could be treated and cured by new miracle drugs.

But increasingly, stronger varieties of these venereal diseases became more and more resistant to the new drugs. Doctors say they are now running out of vaccines to protect against certain sexually transmitted diseases.

In 1988 Chicago public health officials reported that a new strain of gonorrhea, resistant to drugs, had been spreading.

The new strain, reported to have originated in Korea and the Philippines, had not yet been reported in other U.S. cities. But Dr. Richard Biek, deputy health commissioner, said twelve cases appeared in Chicago.

Then, another sexually transmitted disease was reported by the Atlanta-based Centers for Disease Control. Chlamydia was described as a venereal disease afflicting as many as thirty million U.S. adults and teen-agers—more than ten percent of our total population.

Chlamydia is transmitted through sexual promiscuity and also through sexual and non-sexual contacts to innocent parties. Unsuspecting spouses may contract the disease from unfaithful mates. Children are infected by their mothers in childbirth or through breast-feeding.

But as devastating as was the increase in syphilis and gonorrhea and the "epidemic" spread of chlamydia and herpes, these were nothing in comparison with the horror to follow.

In June of 1981, a new sexually transmitted disease was reported—*Acquired Immune Deficiency Syndrome (AIDS)*. AIDS is one of the most virulent and lethal infectious agents ever encountered. Following an incubation period which varies with

Cases Of Sexually Transmitted Diseases

Includes: Gonorrhea, Syphilis, Chancroid, Granuloma Inguinale, Lymphogranuloma Venereum, and AIDS

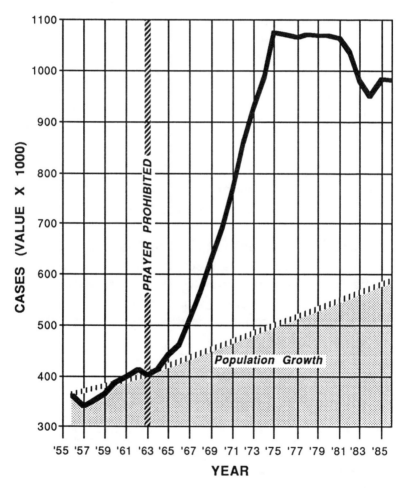

IIIIIIIIII Indicates population growth profile for subject age group.

Basic data from Department of Health and Human Services, the Center for Disease Control, and the Deparment of Commerce, Census Bureau.

different individuals, it kills all of those infected. The virus has already infected over a million Americans and an estimated 10 million people or more worldwide. It is now a global epidemic, and Dr. Alvin Kline of New York University says, ''AIDS is the plague of the millennium.''

There is no safe and effective treatment for AIDS, and no vaccine to prevent it. The AIDS virus invades the nucleus of some of the victim's key white blood cells and passes its genetic material on to the genome (array of genes) within those cells. The victim's immune system is destroyed as a result, so that he becomes vulnerable to a variety of killer-germs. The virus also attacks the brain and central nervous system with lethal effectiveness.

AIDS is not just the result of dirty needles or mass social ignorance. It is the consequence of a culture's willful disregard for God and the determined violation of His Word.

AIDS is not a judgment in the sense of God reaching down with a symbolic club to selectively destroy those who disobey Him. Rather, AIDS is the *natural* consequence when men violate eternal Biblical principles (Gal. 6:7-8).

In the years just ahead, the casualties of AIDS will include:

—*The children of HIV-infected mothers* (Approximately fifty percent of such children will get AIDS themselves).

—*Hospitals and health care facilities* (They will be

overcrowded in a few years and unable to handle many AIDS victims).

—*Insurance companies* (Even if they get relief on AIDS-related claim payouts, it may be "too little, too late" to rescue them from financial disaster).

—*Government agencies* (Welfare, Social Security, Medicare, and Medicaid will be overburdened).

—*Business and industry* (will lose some of their most productive wage-earners, planners, and executives).

—*Education* (Many school systems will be torn with controversy with regard to establishment of "AIDS policies").

There is no question that AIDS, riding on the "free sex" tide instigated by Humanism, will have a monumental effect on the entire civilized world and will forever alter the course of human history.

New Age Delusion

Secular Humanism is atheistic and atheism, in time, will give way to despair. Atheism is contrary to the human spirit. *Men want to believe.*

So, why not create a god for Humanism?

Some Humanist thinkers have adopted the pantheistic "all is God" idea; others create a god in their own image and declare "humanity is God."

The "human potential" movement became a collection of "odds and ends of psychoanalysis, Eastern religion, sexual experimentation, and gameplaying," wrote Alvin Toffler. This is the basis of what is now called the *New Age movement*.

The widespread popularity of new cults and religions testify to secular man's eagerness to believe in *some* kind of god.

"New Age" philosophies allow the Humanist to keep all his evolutionary ideas, and still cling to some idea of divinity.

In the 1970s, *gurus* came from India with a following that included a number of Western pop culture celebrities, which gave the movement a certain credibility. The Asian immigrants introduced Buddhist and Zen philosophies.

Occultists, psychics, and so-called mystics began to flourish as part of this "New Age of Aquarius."

The New Age "consciousness," wedded to basic Humanism, became a movement, was given credibility, and was promoted by the mass media and the entertainment industry.

Television newscasters, writers, and TV hosts used "loaded" terms to discredit Christians and Christian vocabulary. Labels such as "right-wing," "uptight moralist," "fanatical," and "puritanical" were used to belittle Christian spokesmen and groups. But they did not use such negative or loaded terms to describe the views of Secular Humanists, who were always presented as more tolerant and enlightened.

Many of the new converts to the counter-culture were "dabblers," usually teens or people in their early twenties. The satanic influence was evident in their music, jewelry, dress, games, and films. But as they were drawn more and more into Satanism, it was no longer a casual fad for them.

The cult leader and mass-murderer, Charles Manson, was said to be heavily moved by satanic impulses. Manson believed he had reached a state of consciousness beyond morality. Eastern religions tended to exert the same influence to confound traditional Biblical morality. Good and evil were hopelessly bound together in a confusing ethic, so it is impossible to "sin."

New Age ideas and seminars have included not only *Fortune 500* companies, but also the U.S. Armed Forces, the CIA, the IRS, and scores of government groups.

The movement's emphasis on *human potential* ("ye shall be as gods") was eagerly "bought into" by corporate America and government bureaucracy.

At a famous Eastern graduate school for business, a seminar syllabus includes meditation, chanting, tarot cards and other "consciousness-raising" techniques.

Bestsellers among the top ten nonfiction books of the past several years have included numerous books preaching the occult. One, by actress Shirley MacLaine, even became a five-hour ABC miniseries, dealing with reincarnation and supernatural occult phenomena.

A California housewife claims to share her

body with an "entity from the Seventh Dimension." This "entity" possesses the woman's faculties and body as a "channel." Channeling is a New Age term for spirit possession. A human permits a demonic spirit to invade his body to control him. The woman holds seminars and retreats. This "entity" (again through the housewife) tells listeners, "I am an enlightened entity, and I come to you from the brotherhood of light."

Another woman, a forty-year-old, claims she is the embodiment of a man some 35,000 years old.

The pagan, occult base from which the various cults draw their philosophy was originally authored by the devil. The New Age movement simply provided a "hothouse" for all of the new ideas challenging Orthodox Christianity.

The basic beliefs and goals of the New Age movement include:

1) A pantheistic god or human as divine focus;
2) A permissive moral code, especially toward sexuality;
3) An involvement with the occult and spirit possession;
4) A one-world government, economic system, culture, and religion—to be ruled by a godlike modern messiah.

New Age thinkers totally reject Christianity, which they see as the philosophy behind America and the West. "The old ways aren't working anymore" is their explanation, and they blame it on Christian principles, not on the evolutionary theories of Humanism. The New Age ideology has brainwashed an entire generation, eager to marry a "rational Humanist" viewpoint to a spiritual base.

The ultimate end of both Secular Humanism and New Age philosophy is failure—*because neither can give man a reason for living.* The idolatry of Humanism and the fruits of Humanism are self destructive and can flourish only for a season.

Sex and violence, as described in 2 Timothy 3:1-7, frame the idolatry of these "perilous times." Its central altar is well situated in virtually every home in Western society. A form of worship takes place at the shrine of that technological development, TV, with its perverse sex symbols and warped role models.

It is hardly possible for a family to sit down in front of a television set and watch one program on a commercial channel that does not cater to sexual appetites, glamorize violence or immorality, and promote anti-Christian ideas.

U.S. News & World Report (12/22/86) reported that from kindergarten through high school, in just twelve years, children spent 13,000 hours in an academic environment (dedicated to Humanism, we might add).

During that same twelve-year period, youngsters also spend 13,800 hours in front of a TV set. That gives them a combined total of over 27,000 hours of slick, polished, culturally "acceptable" Humanism, expressed in the sick and violent language of the sex revolution and its idolatry.

All this takes place in the child's developmental years—ages five to seventeen—the period of preparation in which they will make the most important decisions in life.

The New Idolatry

In Biblical times, whenever the Hebrews turned away from God, the nation practiced Eastern religions. When the children rejected the faith and values of their parents, idolatry crept in. *Idolatry* is a scriptural term from the Old Testament period, describing the situation when Israel turned her back on God and replaced Him with heathen "idols." The idol was whatever the people worshiped or "lusted after" in place of God.

To an alarming degree today, much of the Church has turned to the idolatry of Humanism. Biblical standards of God's Word have been replaced with the "it really doesn't matter" guidelines of the Humanist society. The Church has lost its consensus and authority on matters of Biblical morality and Godly character.

When the United Methodist Church met in St. Louis for a big ten-day conference, *U.S.A. Today* reported that a key topic was the ordination of homosexuals. One unhappy delegate said, "Homosexuality is a sin, just like adultery. We wouldn't want a minister who was an adulterer, so why would we want one who is a homosexual?"

Divorce, once forbidden to Christian families, is now readily excused in many churches. Dr. James Dobson, a nationally known Christian psychologist, says the divorce rate among Christians is only slightly less than that of the rest of society. Why is it now acceptable?

By the 1980s, the *sex revolution* and its perverse, immoral practices became the most prominent contemporary form of idolatry in Western culture. The sex revolution collectively refers to promiscuity, pornography, easy divorce, abortion, gay rights, sodomy, immoral movies, and television—all violations of the first institution God ordained: the *family*.

Our contemporary idolatry is expressed in this sex revolution. Its symbols of worship and affection entice and seduce. An entire generation is obsessed by sex. If there is any doubt, one only has to look around—at the nearest TV program, magazine cover, movie ad, billboard, public street, or government school curriculum.

Evangelist Luis Palau expresses a timely warning in the Christian film, *God Has No Grandchildren*. He affirms that every generation must choose for itself its own religious destiny. Faith in the living

God, through Jesus Christ, is not passed on to one's children like his race or nationality.

Joshua 24:31 and Judges 2:10 help put this in clear perspective. The first generation *knows God*; the second generation *knows about God*; the third generation *disregards God*.

The Bible outlines seven distinct periods of the Church and illustrates the characteristics of each period. The last of these periods is pictured as describing a people who are "lukewarm, rich and increased with goods," having "need of nothing," but are in reality "wretched, miserable, poor, and blind," in need of "true spiritual riches, purging, white raiment (purity), naked and in need of clothing" (Rev. 3:14-18).

The Church of these last days of Western culture is strongly influenced by the idolatry of affluency, Humanism, and the sex revolution. Today's Church fits the description of the Laodicean Church of Revelation 3:14-18.

But God has provided a better way. When untainted by idolatry, the Christian worldview is supernatural, intensely personal, and highly motivational. It is based on objective truth and is rational as well as practical in its application.

Within the arena of education, God has a better way—the way of dynamic Christian faith applied to, and consistently practiced within, the vitally important area of child training.

In bold contrast to Humanism and its civilization-destroying fruits that have caused the most severe crisis in education in our history, there is the better way that God has provided. The balance of this book will focus on that better way.

GOD'S BETTER WAY

Someone has said the Bible is not a book of suggestions; it is a book of commandments. Obedience to God's commands is the key to a happy, successful life. Which of God's commandments is the most important? Certainly that is the one we would want to know and obey above all else.

The Great Commandment

This question was asked of Jesus, as reported in Matthew 22:36:

Master, which is the great commandment in the law?

Jesus answered him (verses 37 and 38):

Thou shalt love the Lord thy God with all thy heart, and with all thy soul, and with all thy mind. This is the first and great commandment.

In answering the question, Jesus quoted from Deuteronomy 6. A careful examination of this passage yields valuable insights, and some historical background information will make it more meaningful.

Our Western culture sometimes serves as a barrier to the understanding of Scripture, since it was written within an Eastern culture. Because of cultural distinctions, Eastern and Western modes of expression differ.

Many Bible statements are clear to the Hebrew mind because of Jewish background and experience. The same statements require extensive explanation for us, who live in a very different culture. For example, note Psalm 78:5:

For he established a testimony in Jacob, and appointed a law in Israel, which he commanded our fathers, that they should make them known to their children.

The "testimony" or "law" of which the Psalmist speaks is not readily discernible to us. However, for the Hebrew it is clear: it is the law that God "commanded our fathers, that they should make them known to their children." To the Eastern mind, there is only one such law: the one found in Deuteronomy 6, which is an integral part of the Great Commandment.

The Israelites knew the importance of this passage. Their scholars refer to it as the "pivotal passage of Scripture."

Here, then, is one of the most important chapters in all the Bible. Let's look at it in detail, so that we may understand it.

> Now these are the commandments, the statutes, and the judgments, which the LORD your God commanded to teach you, that ye might do them in the land whither ye go to possess it (Deut. 6:1).

The Israelites have just been delivered from Egypt by the power of God manifested in the plagues against Egypt and the opening of the Red Sea. They were spared death by applying the blood upon the doorpost. With these memories fresh in their minds, they are now in the wilderness, on their way to the Promised Land.

At the very beginning of the journey, God spoke to Moses. He said, in effect, "I am going to give you a set of laws. There will be national laws, domestic laws, and moral laws. I am giving them to you so you will know how to live." The instructions continue in verse two:

> That thou mightest fear the LORD thy
> God, to keep all his statutes and his
> commandments, which I command thee.

Who is to keep these laws? In the next phrase,
He explains:

> . . . thou, and thy son, and thy son's son.

Here are three generations. Does that mean
these laws are to be taught for three generations,
and then cease to be taught? No, the Hebrew parent
knew this meant each son had a responsibility to
learn, and each parent and grandparent had a
responsibility to teach. How long was this to be
practiced?

> . . . all the days of thy life.

What benefit would be derived from it?

> . . . that thy days may be prolonged.

Here is the key to long life: keep the principles
of the Word of God. This is true for the individual
and the family (verse two). It is true also for any
nation, as God reveals in verse three:

Hear therefore, O Israel, and observe to do it; that it may be well with thee, and that ye may increase mightily, as the LORD God of thy fathers hath promised thee, in the land that floweth with milk and honey.

For a nation to be great economically, politically, culturally, legally, agriculturally, and militarily, it must keep and obey the Word of God. These principles must affect the law and culture of a land in order for it to be great and prosper. This is why America has been blessed in the past. As our nation obeys these commands, it will be blessed. If it ignores them, blessing will be withheld. Western man must return to the Word of God, bring unscriptural practices to a halt, and return to the Bible as the sociological basis of our culture.

Verses 4 and 5 begin the "pivotal passage" of Scripture. They are familiar, for they are often quoted:

Hear, O Israel: The LORD our God is one LORD: And thou shalt love the LORD thy God with all thine heart, and with all thy soul, and with all thy might.

With our Western mentality, we think this is the sum total of the Great Commandment. We have often heard this much, and no more. So in our thinking the Great Commandment begins and ends with these words.

However, the Hebrew mind does not respond in this manner. There are no periods, question marks, or commas in the Hebrew language. How, then, can they tell when a sentence ends? They know by the grammatical construction of the writing. A Hebrew sentence was not short and simple like most of ours are in English. It could be more like a paragraph, especially if it was of great importance. That is the structure of this passage. The sentence begins with verse 4 and does not end until verse 12.

This can be seen even in the English translation. Mentally remove the punctuation marks, and the flow of the sentence may be seen by the use of the conjunction "and." Each verse, from 5 through 11, begins with this word. It tells the reader to keep going, that he has not yet reached the end. Look at the passage and note the number of times the word "and" occurs.

And thou shalt love the LORD thy God with all thine heart, **and** with all thy soul, **and** with all thy might.

And these words, which I command thee this day, shall be in thine heart:

And thou shalt teach them diligently unto thy children, **and** shalt talk of them when thou sittest in thine house, **and** when thou walkest by the way, **and** when thou liest down, **and** when thou risest up.

And thou shalt bind them for a sign upon thine hand, **and** they shall be as frontlets between thine eyes.

And thou shalt write them upon the posts of thy house, **and** on thy gates.

And it shall be, when the LORD thy God shall have brought thee into the land which he sware unto thy fathers, to Abraham, to Isaac, **and** to Jacob, to give thee great **and** goodly cities, which thou buildedst not,

And houses full of all good things, which thou filledst not, **and** wells digged, which thou diggedst not, vineyards **and** olive trees, which thou plantedst not; when thou shalt have eaten **and** be full; Then beware lest thou forget the LORD, which brought thee forth out of the land of Egypt, from the house of bondage (Deut. 6:5-12).

That is *one sentence!* In it, God states the principle; then He expands it; then He illustrates it; then He gives the promise of blessing for keeping it, and finally, the promise of judgment for disobeying it. In the Hebrew language, it is one long sentence.

Did you notice the number of ''ands'' in the passage? There are twenty of them. Not that the number is important, but they illustrate a principle. It is the contextual principle. In the context of the Great Commandment, God gives the command to *love* Him—with all of our heart, soul, and might. How do we do this? We learn to love God by understanding the Bible.

We cannot truly love people until we know them. Everything we know about God comes primarily from the Bible. We then demonstrate that love by the way we serve Him, give to Him, witness for Him, and praise Him. It is the things we do which demonstrate how much we love God. In the context, we are commanded to love Him " . . . with all thine heart, . . . soul, and . . . might. *And these words*, which I command thee this day, shall be in thine heart: *AND* thou shalt teach them diligently unto thy children. . . . "

It is all tied together. The command is to love the Lord and to put His Word into our heart and life and then to put His Word in the hearts and lives of *the next generation*. And it is to be taught "diligently." What does this mean? In the very next phrase, God explains and illustrates what He means:

> . . . and shalt talk of them when thou sittest in thine house, and when thou walkest by the way.

In other words, whether we are in the house or

out of the house, we should be teaching our children the principles of God's Word.

> . . . and when thou liest down, and when thou risest up.

These words demonstrate how important it is to read and understand every word of Scripture. Deuteronomy 6:6 and 7a have often been referred to as the "Sunday school proof text." Many churches even put them on bulletin boards. But the phrase above shows it is much more than a Sunday concept.

If the Scripture said "when thou risest up and when thou liest down," the Hebrew would think of the Sabbath, or Saturday. But God did not say it that way. He said, " . . . when thou liest down and when thou risest up." It means we are to do this (teach diligently) when we *go to bed* at night, and when we *get up in the morning.*

> And thou shalt bind them for a sign upon thine hand.

Have you ever needed to write a note to remind yourself of something but had no paper? If you're like me, you probably took a pen and wrote in the palm of your hand. After all, the ink will wash off. But the important thing is, no matter where you go, your hand goes with you. There is no possibility of "losing" your note when it is written on your hand. Our hands are always with us, and any message written on them is constantly before us. That is what God means by teaching the Word of God "diligently"—to keep it constantly before our children.

> ...and they shall be as frontlets between thine eyes.

What are frontlets? The Scriptures refer to them in connection with the exodus of the Israelites out of Egypt. They could have been some kind of head decoration or ornament worn on the forehead. The idea is that each time the children saw the frontlets on their parents, they would be reminded of God's principles and commands.

Another possibility is that frontlets were something like the "blinders" farmers used to put on horses or mules to keep their eyes from distractions.

God knows it is critical that children are trained in His Word. Therefore, He emphasizes that they must be taught all day, every day, in every way. The importance of building Biblical principles into the lives of our children cannot be overemphasized.

The Bible is the most important book in the world. We are to write it in the hearts and minds of the next generation, the next one, and the next one.

When does this critical instruction begin? When

should a child begin to be taught diligently, daily and deliberately? Does it begin in high school or college? Does it begin in junior high, elementary school, or kindergarten? The Bible answers the question in Isaiah 28:9:

> Whom shall he teach *knowledge*? and whom shall he make to understand *doctrine*? them that are weaned from the milk, and drawn from the breasts.

Knowledge has to do with life in general, and doctrine has to do with religion. Both are to be taught, beginning at the time the child is weaned. How old is that? It may be as young as six months or as late as two years. A good average is about one year old. So, from the time the child is about one year, we should begin by teaching "knowledge" and "doctrine." That does not mean that we hold a baby in our arms and quote Einstein's theory of relativity or a quadratic equation. What does it mean? The answer is found in the next phrase, verse 10:

> For precept must be upon precept, precept upon precept; line upon line, line upon line; here a little, and there a little.

Instruction must be simple and repetitious. It begins with the simple and moves to the complex by building line upon line.

Train Up a Child

How is the child "weaned?" This is answered in the passage of Scripture that is the most famous verse in the Bible on child training:

Train up a child in the way he should go: and when he is old, he will not depart from it (Prov. 22:6).

Here again, Hebrew thinking can be seen in contrast to Western thought. The philosophy of a well-known doctor, adopted by a generation of parents, was "Train up a child in the way he *wants* to go." No wonder that doctor, in later years, apologized for his teaching. The Scripture tells us to train the child in the way he *should* go, not in the way he *wants* to go.

No doubt every pastor has had parents come to him with hearts broken over wayward children. A mother came to me one day when I pastored a church in California. She said, "I want you to pray for my grown children. When they were little, we had them in church every time the doors were opened. Now that they have gone off to school, they have drifted away from the Lord and they are sowing their wild oats. But I know they are going to come back someday, just like God said they would, and I want you to pray for them."

I said, "Of course I will pray for them. I want to see them come back, too. But what Scripture are you referring to when you say God said they would come back?"

She quoted Proverbs 22:6. Like many good people, she believed it meant that if we do a pretty good job with our children, they may go into a life of sin, but they will eventually come back to the Lord. There is a problem with that; it is not what this passage teaches!

In the Hebrew language, the verse literally says, " . . . *while he is growing old,* he will not depart from it." The concept is not that the child will depart and then come back. It says the child *will not depart* as he is growing older.

We live in an age in which pastors, deacons, and committed Christians are crying themselves to sleep at night because of wayward sons and daughters. They quote Proverbs 22:6 and ask, "What has happened? Have I lost my children? Is this verse true?"

Yes, the verse is true, but we have misunderstood it. The fault is not with the Bible. The fault is with us. The promise in Proverbs 22:6 is a "conditional promise." That is, a certain condition must be met before the blessing can be given. What is the condition? We must "train up the child in *the* way he *should* go." What does that mean?

It was an attorney, Dr. David Gibbs of the Christian Law Association, who explained it to me.

One day he said, "Do you know what the first word 'train' in that passage means?"

I confessed I did not.

He continued, "It did not come from a university or a dictionary. When Solomon selected the word, he took it from a Hebrew mother's vocabulary. It was a word that any untrained, unlearned Hebrew mother would understand, for she used it in weaning her baby.

"Remember, you start training a child when he is 'weaned from the milk,' and this word describes how they did that. In Hebrew, the word 'train' means 'to touch the palate.' The Hebrew mother put some food on her finger, touched the child's palate, and he would automatically swallow."

The more you think about that, the more it makes sense. The palate is the soft, upper portion on the roof of the mouth that extends back to the uvula, the little piece that hangs down at the entrance to the throat. Touching the palate causes a natural swallowing reaction. It was this method that Jewish mothers used in weaning their children.

Again, the difference in the Eastern and Western cultures is evidenced. We wean our children by opening a jar of strained baby food, taking a small spoonful and putting it in the baby's mouth. He usually keeps a little in his mouth and spits the rest out. We scrape it off his chin and start the whole process over again.

The Hebrew mother did not have a jar of

strained baby food. She strained it by chewing it herself; then she put a small amount on the tip of her finger. She got the baby to smile, then put her finger on the palate, and the child automatically swallowed the food—all of it.

This is the first lesson in life that a child learns—how to eat solid food. The principle the Bible is teaching in Proverbs 22:6 is that from the *very first lesson*, the touching of the palate, the parent begins to train the child.

Notice further that the child is to be trained "in the way he *should* go...." That is *inclusive* of all the commandments, statutes, and judgments of the Lord. It is *exclusive* of anything that is not consistent with the Bible. Is there scriptural proof for that statement? Look at Proverbs 19:27, which was written before 22:6:

> Cease, my son, to hear the instruction that causeth to err from the words of knowledge.

Not only is the child to be taught all the principles of Scripture, but he is to be shielded from anything that is *contrary* to the way he should go. Does that mean he is not to be exposed to just a little bit of Humanism, a little bit of evolution, or other unscriptural concepts? That is exactly what it means! It says, *"cease to hear it!"*

The psychologists, psychiatrists, and educators will respond, "You will warp his personality.

He needs to know about those things so he will be socially well-rounded. Do you want to put him in a 'hot house?'" Have you ever heard something like that? When my oldest child, Melody, was old enough to start school, I looked for a Christian school. A friend said, "You mean, you want to put her in a hot house?"

That sounded so intimidating! I could just picture my little girl, sitting there all day long, sweating and suffering. Then one day I asked a horticulturist the purpose of a hot house. He told me, "That's where we develop our best, most exclusive, valuable, and expensive plants."

That is the principle. Delicate, valuable plants are not put on the hillside where they are exposed to damaging wind, rain, heat, and other elements. They are first put in the "hot house" where every element is carefully controlled, and as near a perfect environment as possible is provided. Then they are transplanted when they are strong and mature.

When God told us to cease from hearing instruction that causes us to err, He used imperative sentences—sentences that command.

Train up a child in the way he should go.

Cease, my son, to hear the instruction that causeth to err from the words of knowledge.

Learn not the way of the heathen (Jer. 10:2).

Do you think God would have given the Israelites such an important command, called the Great Commandment, and then ordered them to get their children up in the morning, wash their faces, feed them breakfast, put on their clean, pressed clothes, put a sack lunch in their hands, and send them back down the path to school in Egypt?

There are parents who believe the Bible and who love the Lord, yet each morning send their children into a school system that has completely excluded God and the Bible from it. God clearly commands that we are to train our children diligently and daily in the principles of the Word of God. Yet countless Christian parents send their children each day into an educational system that opposes those very Scriptural principles.

These parents do not act out of rebellion but out of ignorance. But God is shaking the Church in America today with the principles of His Word. The time of ignorance is becoming a thing of the past.

Look at Colossians 2:8:

Beware lest any man spoil you through philosophy and vain deceit, after the tradition of men, after the rudiments of the world, and not after Christ.

How can we be "spoiled"? This is the word that is used when a conqueror takes the spoils of war, when he takes what is valuable away from the vanquished.

Now, what is the most valuable thing you have that can be spoiled? It is your children, your heritage. All through the Bible this can be seen: "Beware lest any man spoil you. . . . "

How? "through philosophy and vain deceit," such as Humanism, or "after the tradition of men," like the teaching of evolution.

Some parents have said to me, "We send our children to the public schools to be missionaries." What really happens is that we send our canaries to teach the sparrows how to sing, and our canaries come home chirping like the sparrows.

We have nearly lost an entire generation by letting the Humanists do the educating and the training. We preach on Sunday, then turn our children over to a pagan system that teaches contrary to the Bible the rest of the week.

God repeats the principle of separation from evil all through the Bible.

Do *your* kids know what is good and what is evil?

> I would have you *wise* unto that which is
> *good*, and *simple* concerning *evil* (Rom.
> 16:19b).

This should put to rest the foolish idea of the modern world that we should teach children good and evil, truth and error, right and wrong, and let them make up their own minds. That is Humanism in its worst form. This idea originated from Satan in the Garden of Eden. God had told Adam and Eve not to eat of the tree of the knowledge of good and evil. Then Satan invented the lie that is still perpetuated today:

> For God doth know that in the day ye eat thereof, then your eyes shall be opened, and ye shall be as gods, knowing good and evil (Gen. 3:5).

From then until now the idea has been handed down that we must instruct children in good *and* evil. Scripture says, "Train up a child in the way he should go...." It is not necessary to give a child a course in the effective art of sinning. He will pick that up with no help from us!

Our objective is to keep children *from* the "garbage" and hellishness that is destroying a generation of young people in our country.

A child's mind does not have to be dragged through the gutter for him to be educated. This satanic philosophy of *exposure* has nearly destroyed our educational system.

A pastor came to me one day and laid a stack of material on my desk. As I read it, I could hardly believe what I was seeing. These were textbooks from a junior high school in Florida. They contained sentence after sentence of the lowest four-letter gutter words. It was absolutely filthy.

The pastor told me how he and thirteen other ministers had taken the books to the local superintendent of schools. They thought he would be as shocked as they were and act immediately to remove such filthy material from the classrooms.

Instead he said, ''Well, how do you expect to educate children unless you expose them to the reality of life?''

That is not education! That is perversion, and it has helped to produce the mess we see today. God said, ''...*wise* unto that which is *good*, and *simple* concerning *evil*.'' We do not have to drag a child's mind through the gutter to educate him.

''Knowing good from evil'' is not ''knowing good and evil.'' We must not expose and corrupt a child contrary to God's Word. To do so is destructive. Our nation's schools are living proof of that.

What happens if we don't obey the commandment to ''Train up a child in the way he should go?'' What will happen then?

Without consistent ''daily in the temple'' teaching of our children, this is what we can expect:

- Children will become sexually active by their high school years.
- They will probably experiment with drugs as well as sex.
- They will consciously reject God and Biblical values.

- Their philosophy and thought will be Humanistic.
- They will receive an education based on relative standards.
- They will reject absolute morals.
- The quality of education will be the worst in generations.

If children are trained in what is wrong as well as what is right, if they are exposed to the lies as well as the truth, they will be confused. We must train them in the way which they *should go*, to make them wise to that which is good. And we should never expose them to evil. If we expose them to that which is good, they will be able to discern sin and error a block away.

A great many college graduates and teachers across this nation know that this is true, but they are reluctant to face what they realize is a scriptural truth. I can sympathize because I, too, was a Humanist. I was trained just as most of them have been trained. How tragic that we have almost destroyed a generation of young people because we were taught that dragging their minds through the gutter and exposing them to evil is the way to educate them.

Yet, these self-appointed "sophisticates" point their fingers at us for putting our children in Christian schools. They are aghast that we put them in "hot houses" where they sing hymns and quote Scripture each day. They tell us, "They will not be able to perform in the real world." The evidence, however, refutes their claim.

Thousands of students graduate from Christian schools each year and attend hundreds of colleges and universities of every description. They function in the upper portion of their classes and consistently score high on course exams. They demonstrate that youths do not have to be exposed to evil in order to function in society.

Government agencies report that fifteen percent of public school graduates are functional illiterates, that twenty-five percent get drunk an average of once a week, that property damage to schools is over $500 million a year, that teachers are mugged and raped, and that armed guards have little capability of protecting all the students and teachers.

Yet, by way of contrast, each year reports come in from Christian schools where over a million children are getting a superior education. In these schools, teachers are not mugged, schools are not vandalized by their students, and drunken parties do not exist.

Christian young people have more character, more stamina, more creativity, and more initiative than their counterparts because they know right from wrong on the basis of being trained in what is "right." They are demonstrating that a generation trained with Biblical principles will make the "real" world what it ought to be. Rather than conform to Humanism, Christian-trained youth use their influence to bring culture into conformity with Biblical values. That's what true education is supposed to accomplish.

Be Not Conformed

The Bible teaches that we are not to be conformed to this world, but rather are to be "transformed" by the renewing of our minds.

What is the "good" that parents want their children to know? Is there a list of things parents should teach children in order to fulfill this command? Can we know what "the way" is in which we are to train our children? There is such a list, and it is found in Philippians 4:8:

> Finally, brethren,
> whatsoever things are true,
> whatsoever things are honest,
> whatsoever things are just,
> whatsoever things are pure,
> whatsoever things are lovely,
> whatsoever things are of good report;
> if there be any virtue, and if there be
> any praise, think on these things.

Notice the list of virtues to which God would have children exposed. Things that are true, honest, just, pure, lovely, and of good report will develop exemplary lives in a nursery school, an elementary school, a junior high school, a high school, and even college and graduate school. That is a list good enough for any age or any level of education.

God says we are to *think, think, think, think, think, think* on *these* things. This is *"the way"* a child *"should go."* This is the *"good"* of which the child should be knowledgeable. If the heads of children are cluttered with trash, there are a lot of things they need to *unlearn*: things that are untrue, dishonest, unjust, impure, unlovely, and of bad report.

Have you ever bought a new appliance? If so, you probably received a manual with it, which tells all about how to operate the appliance properly and get the most out of it.

Most man-made machines and appliances have a manual to go with them. Follow the manual and get the most mileage, best value, and greatest benefits. The man who built the machine wrote the manual because he knows better than anyone how to use it properly.

God made man, and He wrote a Manual to go along with His Creation.

What parents need to learn in this generation is that God made children, and He wrote the Manual on how to educate them. Enjoying the longest life and the most trouble-free living comes from following the instructions of the Book.

We should not apologize for convictions and principles of education that we get from the Bible when they conflict with Humanistic educators' philosophy. If anything, *they* should apologize, for it is their system that is destroying our young people and producing a generation of functional illiterates, confused and violent rebels, and drug "burnouts."

A certain mother in our church did not have a husband. She worked in a bank during the day, and after work helped her boys clean up the school for payment of their tuition. She went out evenings and sold Avon products. She juggled three jobs so that her boys could have a Christian education.

Christian education does *not* cost; it *pays*. It is not an alternative; it is not a luxury; it is not even just a good thing. It is the *law of God*. It is the law that He commanded His ancient people to obey, and by application He now commands us to obey. It is the Great Commandment. It is God's better way.

But how can Christian education be accomplished in today's world? Numerous practical and highly functional programs have been designed for that very purpose. Alternative Christian education programs are available to parents who want to train their children in Biblical principles. We will conclude this book in chapter seven by reviewing some of these availabilities.

SEVEN

HOPE FOR PARENTS

For many parents it is already too late. Their children grew up in schools dominated by Humanism. The resulting turmoil and problems have created chaos and left the debris of broken families, fractured personal relationships, abandoned faith, and rejected moral values.

Wherever I share the message of this book—whether in churches, school workshops, seminars, or conventions—parents approach me with tears in their eyes and tell me about their son or daughter, a product of a failed school system and a casualty of Humanism. One parent, Shirley, said,

My two girls are lost. They grew up and have no interest in church or things of the Lord. My young son is nine. I found some crude notes in his pocket and couldn't believe what I was reading. He said, "Aw, Mom, that's just how it is."

Biblical Imperative

In spite of the Humanist onslaught and the pervading darkness that has resulted from it, there is hope for parents who will conform to God's plan for educating their children. I make no apology for telling parents: Christian education is not just a good idea or a preferred option. It is a *Biblical imperative*.

Parents can—and *should*—take their children out of the world system and provide them with a Christian education.

We have already learned from the previous chapter that God has given parents the basic responsibility for educating their children. "Education" is the word we use in our culture to describe "life training," or preparing children for life and its choices.

Responsible parents can no longer entrust this responsibility to government schools and the entertainment media. America's founding fathers recognized this fact. Matters relating to education, or the life training of children, were not even mentioned in the Constitution. Such matters were among the precious "rights reserved to the People." Modern parents who think *the Constitution* provides for a free government-financed education as one of the listed "rights" are entirely mistaken.

Our founding fathers wisely gave that responsibility to parents. They recognized that government is not a cultural source. They knew that government cannot give its people a culture or moral values—that it only reflects the will and character of the people.

But the parental *right* to train children may not last. Whenever a people fail to exercise their responsibilities, or if they leave them to others (their government), they lose certain liberties. Parents keep the responsibility to train their children only as long as they claim those rights.

Government bureaucracy, teachers' unions, and "educrats" are taking more and more freedoms and choices from the people. The people have allowed government to tell parents what their children will learn in school, what kind of lessons will be taught, what values and lifestyles will be used as role models, and even what to believe.

While Christians can pray for changes in hopeless, failed government schools, the system itself appears to be here to stay. This thought frightens even many government officials.

The Secretary of Education in every recent administration has wanted change. So have many other leaders. There is one question that I am asked everywhere I go, whether in closed sessions in Austin, Texas or at 10 Downing Street, London:

What will be required to bring about educational reform?

There are four elements that are essential to real educational reform:

Back To Parents

A transition must be made in order to rescue education from the professional "educrats," unions, and monolithic bureaucracies. *Control must be given back to parents.*

Parents are best qualified to act on behalf of their children. They seek achievement and result-oriented methods and want the highest quality education at the most reasonable cost.

But since the turn of the century, parents have been told that "big is better" and consolidation is the best way to run a school system. *Untrue.*

Parents were told that the government could run schools more cheaply and efficiently. *Untrue.*

And parents were told that professional educators could do the job better. *Another myth!*

The "old-fashioned" one-room schools built great character in a dozen *generations* of American history, which in turn provided the leadership to build this great nation. All this was done without "professional" educators and bureaucrats. It was done under the local leadership and control of *parents.* Did it work? It *did!*

Johnny could not only read and write, but he

learned how to purchase items and make change, balance a checkbook—and keep his hands out of the cash register. He learned how to get and keep a job, find a wife, and stay married—and raise children who were taught the same values.

For nearly three hundred years, American parents didn't do such a bad job of educating their children. Is there reason to think modern parents would be any less capable?

In order for parents to control their local schools, however, the finances must come directly from the parents.

But to guarantee reform and improve the quality of their children's education, parents must—through effective economic controls—approve the teachers, curriculum, objectives, and philosophy of education.

Today, parental control of education can only be achieved through private or parochial schools in local communities.

Government financing from tax-collected allocations bypasses local control. A type of tuition tax credit or education vouchers must be given each parent—or directed to the private or parochial school by the parents. Just one thousand dollars per child paid by parents would finance private education and the savings in government education alone could pay off the national debt in a short time.

Privatization would provide quality education through competition. For example, parents could select a school and pay a tax rebated tuition. Or each family could be issued a voucher for each school-age child, and apply the voucher to a private school. Weak schools would improve or disappear (Details in *Let's Save Our Public Schools*, copyright 1983, Published by Accelerated Christian Education, Lewisville, TX). Competition in the free market system would force educators to become productive professionals or go out of business.

Back to God

More than ninety-six percent of all Americans believe in God. That is not just a vocal few—it is an amazing majority of the people.

Once parents regain control, this majority will acknowledge a desire for absolute moral standards, traditional values, Biblical principles of character training, and a Theistic world-view.

Some sixty percent of these parents will want their children to learn basic Christian doctrine—such as the atonement, regeneration, the Christian walk, and the second coming of Jesus Christ.

Interestingly, when this *reality* of Christian teaching is put back into the life training of our children, *accountability* will return to Western culture. Marriages will stabilize as parents apply Bible principles of forgiveness, understanding, and grace. Crime will diminish as courts deal more decisively with criminals.

Many Americans would like to see prayer put

back into the classroom and the Ten Commandments restored as moral guidelines. This would dramatically reverse the ''downhill'' trends which have taken place since 1962 when prayer was removed from our schools.

American school curriculum must be rewritten to reflect Biblical values which place responsibility on individuals for their choices in life.

Back to Basics

Modern education not only removed God and all moral absolutes from the classroom, it also abandoned *basics* and *mastery* in favor of the *theoretical* and the *''socially relevant.''*

''Look and say'' replaced basic phonics, and an entire generation has trouble reading. Government school ''look-see'' reading programs have produced millions of illiterate or ''marginally capable'' children who are now adults, having been promoted through the system without learning. According to the Education Commission of the States, *billions* of dollars are lost because of low productivity, public assistance, and crime. Over half of America's prison inmates are totally or functionally illiterate.

Business and government leaders have learned, perhaps too late, that society demands a meaningful reform of basic educational programs and curriculum.

''*New* English'' and ''*new* math'' have replaced

mastery of the basic concept and *mastery of basic skills*.

"Social promotion" is a failed policy that allows youngsters to pass on to higher grades regardless of whether they are ready. In the past, *learning* and *skill mastery* determined promotion to the next grade level. Social promotion also kills student motivation. In contemporary government schools, students do not have to learn in order to progress in the system.

The American Society for Training and Development says that corporate America will have to spend *$25 billion a year on remedial education* in the years ahead (*U.S. News & World Report, 8/15/88*).

So, even secular educators are saying that a return to basics is absolutely essential. "Back to basics" is critical for educational reform.

Back to the Individual

It was the "consolidation" movement around the turn of the century that began to group children in schoolrooms according to their chronological age.

In 1933, when President Roosevelt ushered in the socialism and welfare programs of his New Deal agenda, at least *half* of America's schoolchildren still attended classes in 150,000 one-room neighborhood schools.

The rather recent popular perception is that this consolidated classroom situation is "traditional" American education. *Not so.*

Traditional American education is not a single large chalkboard at the front of the room, but *individual* slate boards—one for each child.

Traditional American education was not a "lock-step" approach with common age-graded textbooks. Instead, the curriculum included a variety of books and materials, geared to *individual progress*.

Finally, instead of a teacher lecturing to the lowest common denominator of a pupil's intelligence and ability, the traditional teacher spent his or her time helping each student or working with small groups.

The *student* was responsible for his own learning in traditional American schools. Older children learned responsibility, patience, self-denial, and other virtues when they helped younger students. The traditional American school was multi-graded, and each student progressed at his own pace.

The chronological lock-step, teacher-centered, textbook-dominated, "chalk-'n-talk" classrooms began in this century, mainly in the big cities, and the concept spread quickly when the "consolidation" movement marched to the various state capitals.

Then, in the 1960s, with more and more politicizing of education, teachers' unions and educational lobby groups pushed for more appropriations and government controls until they had a monopoly.

The one-room school, with local control, was abandoned for the large consolidated classroom where *learning* was replaced with *teaching* and administrative advantages.

Academic results were exchanged for *exposure* to Humanism.

Individuality was lost to *conformity*.

Parent-controlled local schools were replaced by *adminstrator-dominated school districts*.

But a philosophy that includes "back to the individual" will more effectively bring true educational reform.

In order to bring about true educational reform, the entire American school system must get

Back to parental control,

Back to God,

Back to basics, and

Back to individual learning and motivation.

The conventional government controls and funding prevent any real change from taking place in *public* schools. Businessmen, parents, and honest educators admit that the biggest obstacle to educational reform is entrenched teachers and administrators.

The conventional "chalk-'n-talk" classroom is one of the greatest hindrances to *private* educational reform.

D. Thomas King, project director for the St. Paul, Minnesota, schools, concludes that a "knowledge crisis" exists that is of epidemic proportions because the public education system does not adequately teach and prepare children for life (St. Paul *Dispatch*; 4/3/88).

The combination of Humanistic curriculum, government control, lock-step classrooms, social promotion, and conventional teacher-centered instruction, drastically hamstrings reform efforts. The system is archaic. It needs a major overhaul.

King and a growing number of other educators say the answer is highly personalized instruction for each individual. Students would be responsible for their own learning.

Individualism—and the accountability of individuals—is a Biblical concept. Since the Reformation, Western culture has been guided by the individual "priesthood of the believer" doctrine, under which each person is accountable to God. This concept was the basis of *learning* in the one-room school—with the Bible and a teacher motivated by Theistic principles and values.

The success of the Accelerated Christian Education (A.C.E.) system in more than one hundred countries validates the argument for a *return to the basics*. A.C.E. files include hundreds of testimonials providing proof of not only a quality *Christian* education but also of a superior *academic* education. The A.C.E. curriculum is a Theistic-permeated, computer-enhanced, individualized instructional resource designed for use at the elementary and secondary levels.

Computer-Enhanced Learning

The solutions the most visionary educators are projecting for education in the twenty-first century are already available.

The technology exists to provide highly individualized, interactive computer instruction *now*.

A few years ago, the U.S. Department of Education commissioned a national survey on the uses of school computers. Of the 2,331 elementary and secondary schools that were included in the survey, both public and private, some interesting facts emerged:

- Seven years before the survey was conducted, half of all high schools had no computers.
- At the time of the survey, ninety percent of *all* school children were attending a school with at least one computer.
- The typical high school student could benefit and would use a computer for one to two hours each day.
- Computers are used in three basic areas: regular instruction, remedial instruction, and enrichment.
- So far, computers have had little impact on the government school system as a whole.
- Few schools have financial resources to expand computer use.

- There are not enough computers to allow all students to use them on a regular basis.
- Lock-step classrooms do not accommodate consistent application of computers.
- Schools don't have adequate budgets for hardware, software, and teachers.
- Any change in the teacher-centered system is viewed as a threat to the educational bureaucracy.

Even though some educators and educational societies vocally support such change, it is not likely to happen very quickly. The National Educational Computing Conference at the University of North Texas initiated a gallant effort to make some significant changes.

The dozens of workshops and seminars of similar conferences may be helpful in opening doors to encourage computer-assisted education. But experienced businessmen and concerned parents question the ultimate ability of educational societies to overcome the massive political obstacles of the government-controlled school system.

The *greatest* accomplishments and growth of *computer-enhanced learning* will probably come from a united cooperative effort of the private school sector and private enterprise.

In fact, the Christian school movement already has the edge in that development. The *School of*

Tomorrow, developed by Accelerated Christian Education, provides a revolutionary ''High touch, high tech, high teach'' package of twenty-first century learning.

There are three immediate applications:

1. Home Schooling
2. Local Tutorial or Neighborhood Learning Centers
3. Church-operated Christian Schools

Home Schooling

It is estimated that over 200,000 children are being taught by their parents at home. Partly in response to problems in public schools and partly to fulfill spiritual objectives, a new era of home schooling has emerged. In fact, since 1980 this phenomenon has virtually exploded into being all across the country. And the numbers are growing daily.

National and regional home school conventions, curriculum workshops, and home school publications have all emerged within the past decade. So have home school academies—centralized resource and extension schools where parents can enroll their home-schooled youngsters. Parents are provided with curriculum, test grading, and record keeping services. A complete line of supplies, grade cards, resource materials, and equipment is available. Such academies are found in every state.

Computer enhancement of learning is a natural concept for home school families. This technology has come into being quickly and is growing rapidly. The concept of computer-enhanced individualized learning combines the latest electronic technology with a totally self-instructional, God-centered educational curriculum.

The School of Tomorrow offers the most complete computer-enhanced curriculum available. Children can actually learn on the computer. The concept includes *interactive* audio and videocassette lessons and tests that enable the student and the computer to "talk" to each other.

Computers and available software help students to learn, and *enhance* that learning through audio programs and video presentations that clearly visualize course instruction. In biology, for example, students watch a video lesson about birds, the purpose of their feathers, names of skeletal parts, how birds fly, their place in the ecological chain, and how they reproduce. The students take a test, and the computer lets them know how they did.

If they missed some points, they simply rewind the videocassette and watch the lesson again. When they have *mastered the lesson*, they are encouraged by the teacher or parent and permitted to go on to the next lesson.

Computers even keep track of the students'

test scores and can print out progress reports and grades. Students use computers as "time managers" to keep track of goals and plans.

The system has proven itself in a pilot *School of Tomorrow* project. It is more than a model for the future. It is functioning now, and is available to parents.

Individualized, computer-enhanced learning does *not* require parents to be computer experts or professional teachers. But a computer learning system does allow parents to be as involved as they choose. It is the latest high tech, "hands on" learning system that allows a child to employ his own "computerized teacher." It puts the universe at his fingertips.

Community Learning Center

Christian-based computerized learning concepts can be adopted by anyone who has the vision for educational reform. A businessman, parent, teacher, principal, or Christian layman can start a local *tutorial center* or community *learning center*. Such centers provide the child (or adult) with instruction ranging from a single subject to his *entire schooling*. Math, phonics, and reading skills can be provided to "tutor" students currently enrolled in public schools or children who need individualized attention that conventional private schools are unable to provide.

It is feasible for parents to rent a facility for a

learning center—in a shopping mall, office complex, neighborhood building, or even a storefront—wherever local zoning will permit.

This concept provides for the same kind of individualized instruction as home schooling to be expanded, with a creative action plan, into a vital, productive program. Computer-enhanced, individualized Christian curriculum enables teachers, parents, or businessmen to start schools based on the old-fashioned one-room school concept of mastery learning.

Church Learning Centers

The Great Commandment (Deut. 6) places the responsibility for a child's life training on the family. Parents are charged with the ultimate responsibility for educating their children, but they can *delegate* parts of this responsibility to the local church, since the local church is a "family of families," with the same values.

The local church also has the primary responsibility for the dissemination of God's teaching (the Great Commission)—"Go ye therefore and *teach* all nations." The word *teach* is the only imperative in the Great Commission passages. It means much more than to teach people about the Bible. Literally it means "to disciple" or "make disciples."

Parents are to disciple their own children—"daily in the temple" as the Old Testament teaches. The Great Commission provides a practical New Testament fulfillment of the imperative for families.

It's a contradiction that *parents* should "disciple" *the world* while permitting the anti-God disciples of Mann and Dewey, of the Humanist Revolution, to "disciple" *Christian children* for the New Age religion.

If the purpose for the ministry of the Church is "Teaching them to observe all things whatsoever I have commanded you" (Matt. 28:20), then this is a full-time ministry of the church. The Commission includes all "the nations" of the world, but is to begin at home.

Christian education *begins* with the discipling of our own youth, within our own church congregations—before it is to go "into all the world."

Wise pastors are catching the vision to make Christian education a central part of the local church ministry. Since 1970, over fifteen thousand Christian schools of one type or another have opened in America. Concerned parents are becoming involved with churches that are recognizing the Biblical imperative of Christian schools.

Parents are once again assuming their God-given responsibility, and churches are reclaiming their tradition of a Bible-based education. A recent letter from a Christian school principal, who was once a government school principal, underscores the need:

A number of years ago the National Sunday

School Association reported that 70% of the Christian children, who attend public schools, drop out of church between the ages of 12 and 17. Of college students living on campus at secular colleges and universities, 90% drop out of church the first semester.

It is not an exaggeration to say that millions of children from Christian families are being sacrificed on the altar of secular Humanist education.

Clint Behrends, principal of Columbia Heights Christian Academy of Longview, Texas, observes:

Many Christians use Matthew 5:13 ("Ye are the salt of the earth") to defend their children being in public schools. It would appear they've forgotten the second portion of this Scripture, ("but if the salt has lost his savour . . . it is . . . good for nothing"). In public schools our children are being desensitized in their formative years by sending them day in and day out to a system that teaches them contrary to Scripture.

Behrends adds,

If pastors followed the same logic in their Sunday morning services, bringing in the leaders with divergent beliefs...teaching such subjects as safe sex, abortion, homosexuality and evolution, congregations would be up in arms.

We do not want to create the impression that all public schools are totally corrupt and that all Christian schools are perfect. But as a general rule, public schools teach contrary to Christian values and beliefs, while Christian schools are guided by educational philosophies based on Theism.

Clint Behrends concludes,

Individuals who endorse the view that a secular environment will strengthen a child by forcing him to stand up for his own beliefs simply do not understand the Scriptural contradiction that implies. The Word does *not* say "train up a child in the way he should not go and he will be made strong by it." Christian schools offer more than simply an alternative; they give some clear answers for Christian families.

This Christian school principal has put his finger on the central issue—that of prohibiting Humanism from shaping the thoughts and actions of God's people.

Christian parents need to encourage their pastors to start Christian schools in local churches.

The continuing risk and exposure of children to anti-Christian teaching must end. Otherwise it will continue to weaken the body of Christ, conforming it more and more to secular standards.

Perilous Times

Humanism is the basic anti-Christian doctrine and philosophy. Its basic premise is: "There is no God!"

Communism is the political expression of Humanism.

Evolution is the scientific expression of this secular faith.

Relativism is the expression of Humanism in law, economics, and education.

Satanism, drugs, witchcraft, the occult, and *sinful worldliness* are the expression of it in religion.

Immorality, abortion, AIDS, suicide, violence, crime, and *divorce* express Humanism in society and culture.

We *do* live in "perilous times." It's ironic that during this same period we have more educational programs, more academic institutions, more teaching personnel and students, more resources and libraries, and seemingly limitless computerized research. It would seem that men would have all of the answers.

Yet they have been "ever learning and never able to come to a knowledge of the truth."

Everything in this book that describes our

"perilous times" can be associated directly with the revolution of secular Humanism on a world-wide scale.

Humanism seeks to dethrone God.. Many believe we are in the final stages of preparation for the ultimate confrontation. A collision between the two forces—God and Antichrist—is inevitable. The battle can be traced as far back as Eden.

Humanism is simply today's version of mankind's second oldest faith—"ye shall be as gods." It is the perverted *counterfeit faith*.

> This know also, that in the last days perilous times shall come.

> For men shall be lovers of their own selves, covetous, boasters, proud, blasphemers, disobedient to parents, unthankful, unholy,

> Without natural affection, trucebreakers, false accusers, incontinent, fierce, despisers of those that are good,

> Traitors, heady, highminded, lovers of pleasure more than lovers of God;

> Having a form of godliness, but denying the power thereof: from such turn away.

> For of this sort are they which creep into

houses, and lead captive silly women laden with sins, led away with divers lusts,

Ever learning, and never able to come to the knowledge of the truth.

...these also resist the truth: men of corrupt minds, reprobate concerning the faith.

But evil men and seducers shall wax worse and worse, deceiving, and being deceived (2 Tim. 3:1-8, 13).

"Perilous times" *are here.* Notice that this Biblical passage describes a Humanist revolution. "Evil men" are committing all sorts of unbelievable sins, and things are becoming increasingly "worse and worse."

And without a return to true education based on Biblical values, believers can expect that things will become even more sinful, violent, depraved, and lawless as secular Humanism pervades Western culture and infects other societies as well.

Hope for Parents

Fortunately, parents today need not send their children down the slippery slide of Humanism to the moral abyss of Egypt for an education. Christian education is available today—and it is ready to meet the spiritual and academic needs of families.

Our only hope while we remain on this planet is to confront the evils of these perilous times. Strategists tell us that in most conflicts or contests, the best defense is a good offense.

Our most effective retaliation to global secular Humanism is in obeying both the Great Commandment and the Great Commission.

We have in these twin imperatives all that is necessary to bring our children to faith, teach our families God's truth and precepts, and disciple our community to live by Theistic values.

Christian education offers a bright new hope for parents—and that hope will become reality through godly parental initiative in planting more and more new schools throughout the world.

Through this means the moral and intellectual basis of civilization will be sustained, and God's good purposes for mankind will continue to be fulfilled, no matter how dark and perilous the times, until our Lord shall return.

INDEX